How To Build A

WEST COAST CHOPPER

KIT BIKE

How To Build A

WEST COAST CHOPPER KIT BIKE

Mike Seate

MOTORBOOKS
INTERNATIONAL

First published in 2002 by MBI Publishing Company,
380 Jackson Street, Suite 200, St. Paul, MN 55101-3885 USA

MBI Publishing Company books are also available at discounts in bulk
quantity for industrial or sales-promotional use. For details write to Special
Sales Manager at Motorbooks International Wholesalers & Distributors,
380 Jackson Street, Suite 200, St. Paul, MN 55101-3885 USA

Library of Congress Cataloging-in-Publication DataAvailable
ISBN 0-7603-1872-7

Edited by Peter Schletty
Designed by Chris Fayers

Printed in Hong Kong

CONTENTS

INTRODUCTION

This early El Diablo chopper features a rare, single-downtube Softail frame, forks extended 12 inches and a wicked, sword-shaped jockey-shifter. While this radically stretched chassis isn't for sale to the general public, creative amateur chopper builders can come close to achieving similar mechanical perfection using their imaginations and lots of sweat equity.

DO IT YOURSELF

What do NBA superstar and L. A. Lakers team captain Shaquille O'Neil, "Matrix" star Keanu Reeves, and rap-rock musician Kid Rock all have in common? Each of these A-list stars is the proud owner of a custom-built West Coast Chopper, a rare, hand-built motorcycle crafted in the Long Beach, California, studio of master builder Jesse James. Besides sharing ownership of some of the most sought-after custom motorcycles on the planet, each of these riders also enjoys a lavish superstar lifestyle, rife with more money than most of us will earn in a dozen lifetimes.

Their rarified status has much to do with owning a genuine West Coast Chopper. The cost of having Jesse James and Co. design and construct a motorcycle to suit an individual's tastes and riding needs can cost nearly $100,000 and take up to two years to complete. That's *if* you can get your name added to the shop's burgeoning waiting list.

Short of launching your own Hollywood film career or somehow acquiring the skills necessary to compete in professional sports, it would seem the road to owning a West Coast Chopper, or any top-flight custom motorcycle, is completely blocked. But unbeknownst to many would-be custom bike owners is the option of the home chopper build. For the past few

Orange ghost flames spread across a House of Kolor Tangelo orange base coat makes the finish on this El Diablo II chopper a knockout. Built for rap-rocker Kid Rock as he joined builder Jesse James for a cross-country ride through Mexico in the documentary film Motorcycle Mania III, *this Softail chopper was constructed with both speed and comfort in mind.*

years, West Coast Choppers has made most of their signature chopper parts, accessories, hard parts, and mechanicals available to the general public, allowing a moderately skilled builder to create a running replica of the motorcycles that helped launch the current chopper renaissance.

The build-it-yourself chopper is far from a new concept. Aftermarket parts firms like California's A.E.E. Choppers, Colorado's Jammer Enterprises, and dozens of others helped fuel the first chopper craze during the late 1960s and early 1970s by manufacturing everything a backyard builder could desire, from complete chopper frames to wild extended forks and sheet metal parts. For the better part of a decade, motorcycle customizers curious about what it would be like to roll down Main Street aboard a stretched-out custom sled have needed little more than a check or money order, a family garage, and a mechanic's toolkit to join the Easy Rider generation.

In time, many of the early DIY chopper kits and accessories proved to be of either substandard quality or of questionable taste. Without the celebrity bike builder culture that drives today's chopper scene, most at-home builders simply designed their customs with a haphazard approach and, as a result, too many riders ended up simply bolting a coffin gas tank, apehanger handlebars or maybe a twisted steel chromed set of springer front forks to an otherwise stock motorcycle. Often the results weren't pretty.

Today's custom chopper enthusiasts benefit from a parts aftermarket that offers items capable of re-creating, in stunning detail, many of the signature creations of builders like Jesse James, Paul Yaffe, Chica, Billy Lane and others. These modern kit bikes were created by the celebrity builders under their guidance and to their own exacting specifications, ensuring that the home-built choppers bearing their names are as close to an in-house custom creation as possible.

Eye-catching custom choppers don't have to cost a mortgage to look cool; this C.F.L. chopper, similar to the one we'll built in this book, is centered around the same rigid chassis now available through Custom Chrome, Inc. Red powdercoated wire-spoked rims are boss and cost far less than expensive billet aluminum rims; dual Cordova exhausts and black anodized air cleaner are West Coast Choppers off-the-shelf items.

With its flush-mounted gas cap, narrow profile and stretched lines, this 3.5-gallon Villain gas tank is a West Coast Choppers original—what you choose to do with yours is a matter of individual choice.

Many riders I've met who've seen my West Coast Chopper have instantly assumed that the flash piece of steel I'm riding must have cost me a re-mortgaging of my family house. Some assume that writing must be a far more lucrative undertaking than most people can easily imagine. Closer to the truth, a builder willing to cut a few corners and scrimp on high-end billet aluminum parts can create a West Coast kit bike for about the same price as a bone-stock new Harley-Davidson big twin.

Sure, a new Dyna Wide Glide or a Super Glide Sport may come complete with a factory warranty, shop support, and road-legal amenities. But visit any

Most of us won't earn enough green in a dozen lifetimes to special-order a custom-built West Coast chopper like this mean, blue and green El Diablo II. Lucky for us, there's the home-build option which can yield some show-winning results for about one third the cost of this $80,000 Softail flyer.

custom bike show or biker gathering and you'll be guaranteed to find a parking lot or convention hall full of Harley riders who've unbolted and tossed away thousands of dollars in stock equipment, parts they've inevitably replaced with aftermarket custom bits. They're all chasing—and often missing—the satisfaction and pride that comes from riding a motorcycle that was designed by an individual, not a marketing committee or focus group. And there's no amount of bolt-on chrome or billet that can make a stocker into a genuine custom. That's something the kit bike builder will know and never forget the first time their new ride is rolled into a crowd of bolt-on customs.

Naturally, a genuine West Coast Chopper conceived and constructed at Jesse James' Anaheim Avenue headquarters will benefit from the sort of spontaneous creativity and one-off detailing that, by nature, doesn't exist on a kit bike. However, an at-home builder can easily invest a little imagination and sweat equity into a chopper project to make even the lowest-buck custom bike into an eye-popping original.

That's basically what this book sets out to reveal to potential chopper builders and custom bike fans: We didn't have an NBA-star's eight-figure salary to work with when we decided to try and build a replica of a West Coast Chopper and, far from the custom bike incubator that is Southern California, we had to rely on the creative skills and idea mill of our principal builder, one Steve Peffer of Pittsburgh's Steel City Choppers.

Don't expect to find this hand-sculpted West Coast Choppers gas tank or the wild, tusk-shaped frame supports down at your local Harley-Davidson dealership, though any moderately skilled mechanic can use one-of-a-kind Jesse James creations like these for template when building their own choppers.

The Z-shaped handlebars are a West Coast signature. They can be custom-built at a custom-built price, or purchased off-the-shelf for the budget-minded home builder.

Peffer, a talented mechanic who has made a name for himself by building choppers with more grit, style, and determination than dollars, proves that kit bikes can yield custom motorcycles as cool and as exciting to ride as a big bucks sled from Jesse James' own hands. After purchasing the chassis and other parts to start this project, I spoke with Jesse and his shop manager Bill Dodge about home project bikes and both were encouraging about the possibilities.

"We actually love seeing what people do at home with our parts because these guys working on a shoe-string budget sometimes have the best ideas. They have to make do without a lot to work with, and that's what choppers are all about," James told me. Encouraging words, to be sure.

The timeless cool of the hardtail California chopper is captured perfectly in this West Coast Choppers-built C.F.L. rigid: Wide Glide forks are extended six inches with an additional 5 degrees of rake in the triple clamps complementing the 38-degree chassis rake.

JESSE JAMES' EL DIABLO LOWRIDER

Owned by drag racer Tom Ianotti, this El Diablo II Chopper is pure West Coast from its hell bent exhaust to its red, anodized six-gun handlebar riders.

One of Jesse's most successful and best-loved motorcycles is a lowrider, not a chopper. *El Diablo*, or "The Devil," combines the flowing, voluptuous lines of classic West Coast Choppers sheet metal with chassis dimensions that make for a ride on par with a production motorcycle. This machine was built during the winter of 1999 and featured on the Discovery Channel's *Motorcycle Mania* documentary, and it's one of the fastest, most comfortable West Coast Choppers ever.

The comfort comes from the shop's Dragon Softail frame. With 38 degrees of rake and a set of Legends air-adjustable shock absorbers mounted horizontally underneath the swingarm, *El Diablo* is smooth enough for an all-day ride or an easy blast along the boulevards. With little in the way of stretch in the frame's backbone or downtubes, the Diablo's center-mounted foot-pegs, low seat height, and two-inches-shorter-than-stock-length front forks make for a motorcycle that turns as sharply as any import sportbike. Jesse was looking to create a gas tank and bodywork with complete aesthetic flow for this machine, he said, so the 4-gallon gas tank's bottom curve tends to share the same arc as the tusk-shaped fender struts and the rear fender. A teardrop-shaped recess graces not only the side of the gas tank, but surrounds the top of the aluminum gas cap as well. One-piece, V-shaped handlebars and a leather-vinyl combination saddle built upon a West Coast Chopper aluminum seat pan sets this beauty apart from the pack.

But, *El Diablo* is no easy chair. Like every other West Coast Choppers' creation, it too boasts a big-inch stroker motor—a Patrick racing 113-ci billet mill that propels *El Diablo* from 0 to

The flush-mounting system on the gas tank of this El Diablo II *Chopper makes for incredibly clean lines.*

Center-mounted foot pegs and controls; 2-inch understock front forks; custom v-shaped welded handlebars.

60 miles per hour in a license losing 4.9 seconds. A top speed of near 140 miles per hour can be achieved with the help of an S&S "D" series carburetor and a set of wide-open Hell Bent exhaust pipes produced in-house via one of Jesse's handmade welding jigs.

Though longbikes and stretch choppers have clearly eclipsed more modest designs like El Diablo, it's still being made at West Coast Choppers in small numbers, proving that some riders will always choose outright performance over style . . . one of the many choices any builder must make.

CHAPTER 1
KITTED OUT

Choosing the parts that will comprise your *West Coast Chopper* can be confusing given the myriad accessories currently on the market. A smart builder, however, will stick with only parts manufactured by Jesse James' shop for the most cohesive look and the most ease of construction. Joe Appel

Among the myriad offerings from aftermarket motorcycle parts houses, kit bikes are fairly plentiful. Firms like Biker's Choice, Phantom Cycle, Paul Yaffe, and Midwest Motorcycle Supply all offer chopper-in-a-box kits for home builders, with the latter even supplying a motor and drivetrain components with their Ultima packages.

The current line of parts that we chose to construct our West Coast Chopper became available in 2001 through a licensing agreement between West Coast and Custom Chrome Incorporated (CCI). Unlike Midwest's chopper kit which provides builders with just about every component necessary to create a chopper except a goatee and dirty fingernails, the Jesse James parts offered through CCI's massive Big Book catalog require the buyer to pick and choose individual parts and accessories when creating a kit bike.

What's offered is not an incredibly wide selection when compared to the prodigious output of custom motorcycles from the West Coast garage. Many of the unusual frame configurations and groundbreaking sheet metal parts lusted after by viewers of Jesse James' weekly Discovery Channel TV series *Monster Garage* have never been offered to the buying public. The tortoiseshell-shaped "Wasp" gas tank that graced the single downtube El Diablo II frame seen on *Motorcycle Mania II*, for instance, can only be attained by having a custom bike built from scratch by Jesse himself, despite frequent requests for copies. But the West Coast-designed parts that have become available

Midwest Motorcycle Supply of Arnold, Missouri are just one of several dozen manufacturers offering big-inch stroker motors to at-home chopper builders. Their Ultima products line offers the aptly-named El Bruto engine in a window-rattling 127-cubic-inch version and this milder 113-inch model. Fully polished and ready to install, the El Bruto needs only a bolt-on charging system to get rolling. Steven Dietz

through CCI do offer builders a ground-floor introduction to the West Coast Choppers stable.

Before deciding to begin our project chopper we asked ourselves a few questions about just what sort of chopper we were interested in building, setting up a budget for parts, labor, and the inevitable cost over-runs. After weeks of planting our noses in parts catalogs and studying photos of West Coast choppers built over the past decade or so, we decided to shoot for two main goals with our kit bike. For one, it had to be relatively affordable to prove that choppers are not necessarily toys for millionaires and master mechanics alone. I've met dozens of young riders in recent years who lust after choppers but have been scared off by the extravagant expense of the parts necessary for building one. Today's custom parts are built to some fairly exacting specifications and, as a result, are labor-intensive to produce and seldom easy on the wallet. However, we figured that by choosing parts from West Coast Choppers on the low-end of the cost spectrum, we could ride away with a bike maintaining all the timeless cool of a Jesse James chopper while still leaving us a few bucks for a round down at the pub when finished in the garage.

Another reason we wanted to use as many genuine West Coast Choppers parts as possible is because we've too often seen poor results of builders who have crafted choppers using a hodge-podge of parts from different builders. We've all seen the ads placed in local Cycle Trader publications advertising a "Genuine

Biker's Choice supplied this excellent five-speed, close-ratio transmission from Twin Power. The chromed case unit will require only an extended starter shaft to accommodate the Primo 3-inch open belt drive we'll run (which was partially installed in this photo).
Steven Dietz

Jesse James Chopper" only to realize on closer inspection that we're looking at a Chopper Guyz frame with a set of Ness fenders and a Chica gas tank—and, oh yeah, a set of JJ's Hell Bent exhaust pipes.

When spotting a mix-and-match chopper like this at a custom bike show, I often approach the owners to find out why or how they came to mix so many different designer's goods at once. Most will tell you that budget constraints and limited parts availability often contributes to building bikes from whatever parts just happen to be hanging off the local dealers' shelves. One month he may stock sheet metal bits from Rick Doss, but when the money is finally in hand to buy a frame or oil tank, the dealer has switched to another line of parts altogether.

To avoid this, we suggest saving your pennies until there's enough cash in hand to buy all of the parts for a single chopper at one time. That's not an easy course of action as few banks will extend a loan to a grubby chopper builder who won't have a running, street-legal motorcycle to use as collateral for months. And the waiting game can be tough when you want to start piecing together your dream ride right now. But when you pull up to the curb in front of your favorite watering hole on a bike with that unmistakable Long Beach look, you'll be glad you waited.

CHOPPER SHOPPING

Though the West Coast Choppers parts department at CCI offers both a Softail-style version of Jesse James' famous Dragon chassis, we chose a rigid C.F.L. (or Choppers For Life, the name Jesse bequeathed upon this particular style of bike) frame as it costs about $1,000 less than its plush-riding brother. This

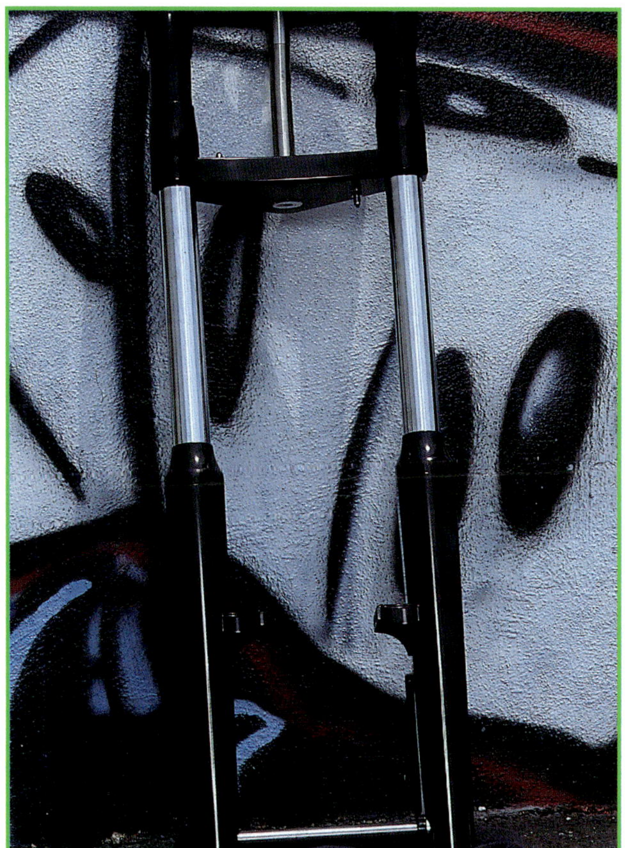

When your chopper will roll without benefit of rear suspension, builders may want to ensure their front end has more than enough damping: this hex-legged, Wide Glide front fork assembly is from California's Perse Performance and is built to some impressive standards. Joe Appel

The internals of the Perse front forks were crafted with assistance from Race Tech who provided heavy-duty springs and cartridge emulators—axle mounts are cleverly hidden beneath a removable shield. Steven Dietz

eliminated the need for expensive suspension parts and maintained our mantra of Keep It Simple. The original California choppers were mostly based on rigid hardtail frames as well so we figured tradition trumped a comfier ride for us this time.

Both frames are designed with similar dimensions including 38 degrees of rake and a 2-inch downtube stretch, plus an additional 1 inch of stretch in the backbone. Both models are made with thick 1½-inch backbone tubing and 1¼-inch tubes throughout. Fracture-resistant box-shaped motor mounts are standard and they can run moderately wide rear tires up to 180 mm (or 5.5 inches in rim width).

Riders opting (as we did) for pure chopper styling can run a chain final drive instead of a toothed belt setup which allows more room at the rear end, accommodating a 200-mm tire with a few simple modifica-

tions. Our chassis kit even comes with one of Jesse's way-cool cylindrical oil tanks with attached battery box and a set of his signature Maltese cross axle covers. The frame's backbone stretch creates a fairly tall engine bay which CCI says will accommodate massively stroked motors as big as 132 cubic inches, but motor selection for this project (which we'll get to shortly) involved much more than just filling a hole in the chassis.

Next on the shopping list was a full set of Jesse James sheet metal body parts. Though the sleek and stretched 3.5-gallon Villain gas tank is perhaps the best-known fuel carrier from the WCC stable, we cheaped-down and purchased one of Jesse's 3-gallon King Sportster tanks featuring a flush gas cap and a filled tunnel that retails for just under $250. We were lucky enough to pick up our parts directly from West

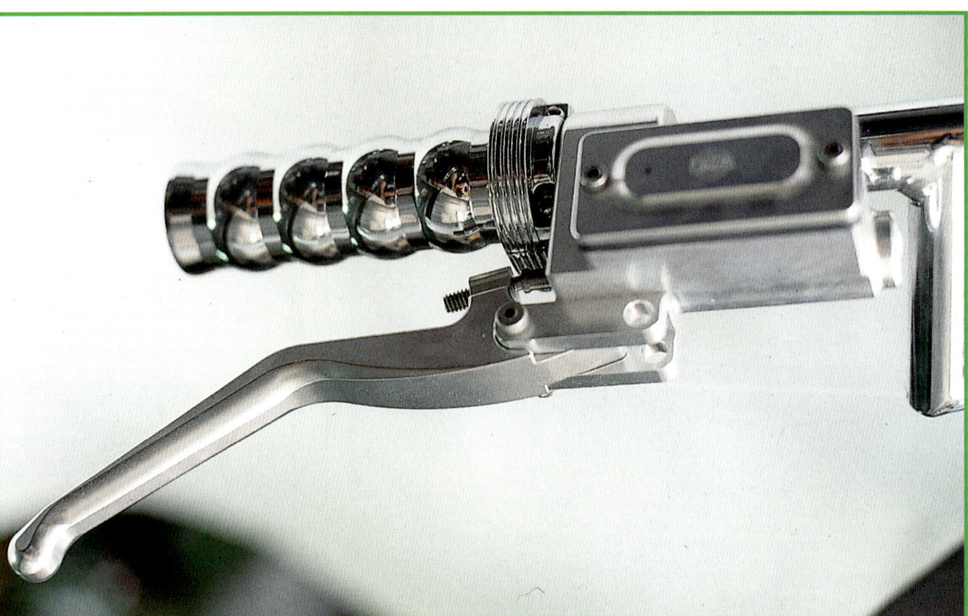

Chrome handgrips are swap meet specials and cost just $30—the single front brake disc will be brought to a halt via this GMA clear anodized master cylinder.

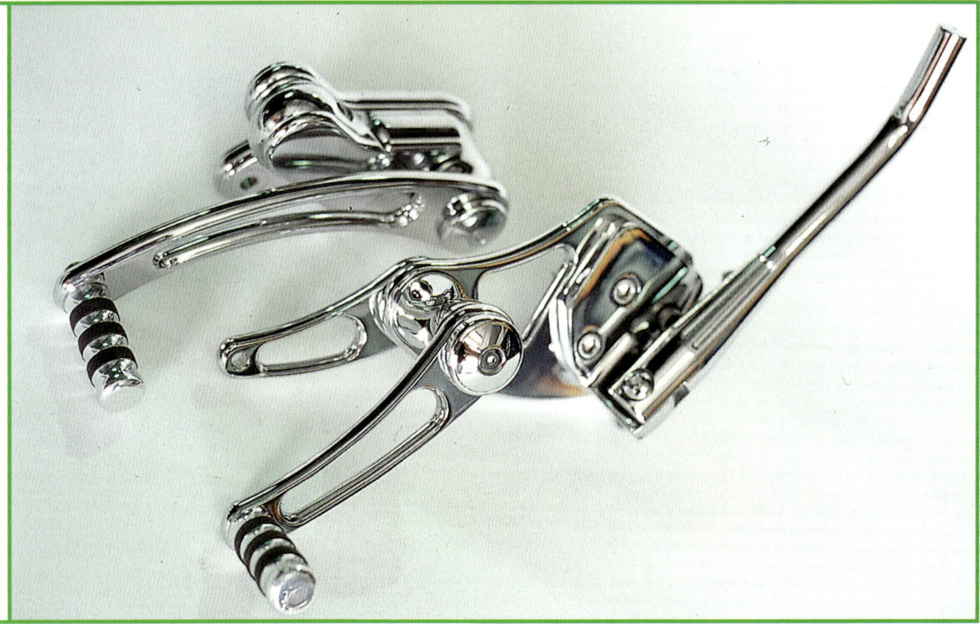

From the Bay Area workshop of legendary chopper builder Arlen Ness come these sleek and highly functional Radius forward controls. Right-side footrest includes an integral master cylinder which helps keep our chopper's rear end uncluttered.

Coast Choppers and had the opportunity to place the Sporty tank along the top frame backbone to see how it fit—perfectly, we found out, as the C.F.L.'s minimalist lines proved a fitting platform for the simple and clean gas tank.

Next came a set of West Coast Choppers fenders, a 9-inch-wide "Two Eight" model for the rear and a swoopy 4¾-inch wide "Diablo" for the front. These fenders are wildly popular for backyard customizers and chopper fanatics alike for their thick steel construction and a system of steel tube bracing running along the underside of each unit that helps prevent vibration stress fractures.

We couldn't complete our own C.F.L. chopper without some of the signature West Coast items like the Maltese cross air cleaner ($529), Hell Bent exhaust pipes ($1,100), and a set of bitchin' .44-magnum handlebar risers ($289).

The high-flow air cleaner is constructed from 6061-grade billet aluminum and will fit most carburetors from the stock Kehins found on a Harley-Davidson powerplant to several S&S car-

Once a West Coast Choppers exclusive part produced one-at-a-time for custom choppers, this cylindrical, 3-quart oil tank and battery box helps make the C.F.L. project a winner. Builders may want to check whether their battery will fit the relativcly shallow box before installation. Steven Dietz

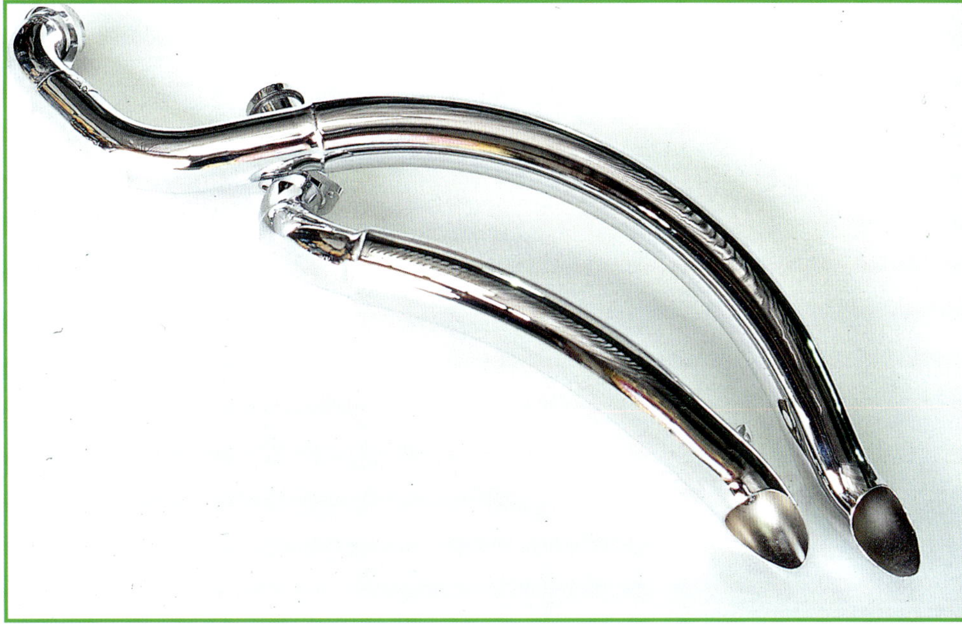

Today, Jesse James has licensed three different sets of his ascending-radius exhaust pipes, all of which feature thick steel wall construction and no mufflers to speak of. We chose the original Hell Bent models. Steven Dietz

buretors, including the big-bore Super "E" and Super "G" series.

The Hell Bent exhaust pipes are one of several models now being offered to at-home chopper builders, including the shotgun-style L.B.C. pipes and the gracefully arching Cordovas. We went with the original Hell Bent after researching some of the first C.F.L. bikes to emerge from the West Coast garage and realizing what a perfect fit they were for a spare, well-balanced chopper. A word of warning: These babies are LOUD with a capital "L" due to a triple-stepped expanding diameter design that allows maximum flow of exhaust gasses—and decibels—at all revs.

Since we decided to have a local shop construct our own custom seat, we wouldn't need to purchase a custom-made seat pan for our ride, though CCI offers one to fit the C.F.L. in their current catalog.

We'd placed a lot of cash into our West Coast parts order, but wcrc still in nccd of a bling'd-out set of rims that would add flash and style to our budget chopper. After soliciting photos and testimonials from riders around the country who've built their own versions of

Weld Industries, long respected for producing high-quality racing rims for cars and light trucks, created these bitchin' Widow model billet wheels. Show-chromed and available with matching rotors, they even matched the groovy little spiderweb frame gusset on our West Coast chassis. Steven Dietz

Jesse James' famous stretch bikes, we noticed that a good many of them chose to scrimp a bit when it came to the wheel department. Most ran simple aluminum rims with stainless-steel or chromed-steel spokes, an option that can save a budget-minded builder a couple grand over the cost of a set of CNC machined billet aluminum wheels.

West Coast Choppers offers their own extensive line of wheels which are as groundbreaking as their motorcycles. However, being fans of the bitchin' spiderweb motif used for the frame gusset on our C.F.L. chassis, we were pretty stoked to find that Weld Industries, a longtime supplier and designer of racing components and custom car rims offers a spiderweb wheel design known as "The Widow" through their Evo series of motorcycle rims. We chose a 21 x 2.15 front model and an 18 x 5.5 rear, with a set of matching brake rotors that really set off the web motif that we'd try to re-create in the custom seat stitching and a few other details. Show-chromed and machined with beautifully cut web patterns in each of the four spokes, the Widow wheels took a good $2,200 out of our budget for a set—plus an additional $399 each for the brake rotors—but it was worth the expense considering what a powerful visual effect a set of well-made rims has on a chopper.

Much the same could be said of front ends, a component that will hang up the planning stages of building a chopper for longer than a maxed-out Visa card. That's because so many options are available, from springers and girders, with their relatively spindly diameter tubing and near-rigid suspension travel, to heavyweight billet forks in mid-glide and wide-glide configurations, and even road-racing style forks with upside-down sliders.

Because the West Coast Choppers C.F.L. frame was designed with a relatively modest 38-degree rake, the motorcycle, despite being a chopper, was made to steer quickly and offer similar handling to a Harley-Davidson Sportster, according to Jesse James. The first C.F.L. featured footpegs that were mounted not forward of the frame but in the same position as those on stock Harleys, adding balance and swift steering. The forks on this lime green machine were also built for speed, not style, extending only four inches longer than stock.

We approached master fork designer and former aerospace engineer Joey Perse about the best front suspension for a rigid C.F.L., and the Colorado techni-cian quickly suggested one of his beefy 41-mm hex-shaped wide glide fork kits. Perse also designs his front ends to contain just the right amount of front wheel trail (a measurement of the distance between a front tire's contact patch with the pavement and the axis of the front wheel) to ensure there's none of that floppy, unsteady sensation often found in forks mounted to even the most mildly stretched chopper frames. He had us measure the distance from the frame neck to a spot on the garage floor where the front axle would be once the front wheel was installed and then made a few quick calculations resulting in his designing a set of forks five inches longer than stock and a pair of custom triple trees containing an extra five degrees of rake to reduce wheel trail considerably.

With plans to paint the bike a vivid metalflake and flame scheme—like the first C.F.L. ever built, of course—we decided to go with one of Perse's black powder-coated front ends to add a little contrast to a machine that will surely have more than its share of brightwork and detailing.

Making sense out of this pile of multi-colored spaghetti has never been simpler with the advent of complete wiring harnesses like this one from Custom Chrome, Inc. Designed to fit stock Harley-Davidson Softails, these harnesses will slip into a West Coast Choppers frame with a few simple modifications. Steven Dietz

On sale to amateur chopper builders since 2000, the C.F.L. or Choppers For Life chassis is also available in the Dragon Softail version with either 1 inch of backbone stretch and 4 inches in the downtubes, or similar to this more conservative model featuring 1 inch in the backbone and 2 inches of stretch in the front downtubes. For bargain hunters, the rigid model is a sure bet for just $3,500. Joe Appel

The Perse forks, which include brake mounting points for a single left-side disc setup (running a pair of front discs seemed a little costly), retail for around $3,200 and, to be sure, there are plenty of cheaper options available to the home builder. But without any suspension damping at the hardtail rear end of our chopper, we felt it was impossible to overcompensate when it came to choosing a front end.

To that point Perse's forks aren't just pretty, they're built to a level of performance that would flatter a crew chief in an AMA Superbike paddock. The fork springs are heavy-duty units from high-performance firm Race Tech and have adjustable spring preload rates for extra bumpy roads of long, cross-state hauls. Hidden axles and internal brake-line routings make

for a good-looking and functional fork.

This is an all-important part of planning your at-home West Coast Chopper, as front fork length and design will very much dictate the type of riding you'll be able to command of a finished motorcycle. We suggest drawing a few sketches of what you'd like your chopper to look like, and studying the profile and length of several styles of fork before whipping out the green and making a purchase. We've met some builders who've gone so far as to cut the front ends completely off their C.F.L. frames to re-attach the steering neck with additional rake for the mounting of extremely long chopper forks. While this look is sure to get you noticed, it may end up making what was intended to be a fairly maneuverable chopper into a

That brass Maltese cross label on the frame neck means this chopper will be born with a seriously cool engineering heritage—remember to remove the rivets holding it in place before primer and paint go on! Joe Appel

While the craze among contemporary choppers builders seems to be for ever-fatter rear tires, common sense and rideability told us to stick with real-world wheel sizes. Our Weld Widow rear is an 18x6-inch while the front is a narrow 2.15x21-inch chopper style. Metzeler Sportec radial tires mean comfort and grip even if we get caught in the rain. Joe Appel

machine that goes around corners with all the reluctance of an aircraft carrier! That's also a lot of extra work, requiring extensive welding skills and specialized equipment—not an area we plan to address for a project bike that uses as many simple, bolt-together components as possible.

We spent another three grand or so fleshing out an extensive list of necessaries, including a set of CCI's universal braided-steel oil lines, a set of matching brake lines, a Dyna 2000 ignition module with coil, braided brake lines for both front and rear calipers and a set of Arlen Ness' Radius forward foot controls (which we chose for their sheer beauty) and the unique, internal master cylinder mounted to the brake-pedal mount, eliminating the need for a master cylinder hanging awkwardly from the bike's rear end.

The transmission is a Twin Power five-speed unit ($1,900) in a polished case from Biker's Choice. This veteran aftermarket parts firm has a well-deserved reputation for producing slick-shifting, reliable gearboxes. The transmission, like most of the major components on our chopper, was designed to fit late-model Harley-Davidson Softails and will bolt directly in place on the mounts designed by West Coast Choppers; the RST two-piston rear brake caliper (sourced through CCI for $339 plus $149 for a chrome mounting bracket) was no exception.

We'd spent the better part of a month staring at

We scrimped and saved a few bucks by opting for a simple, chromed steel headlight bucket from CCI which retails for just $144—or about one quarter the price of billet aluminum models. That left us some cash to splash on these bad-assed .44-magnum handlebar risers from West Coast Choppers. Steven Dietz

Thick, 18-gauge steel construction makes Jesse James' fenders a sure bet even for folks just looking to add a little style to a stock motorcycle; brass nameplate rests on the underside of each unit. Joe Appel

Delivered in bare metal, our fenders included a nine-inch-wide "Two-Eight" rear model constructed to match the hidden mounts on our C.F.L. frame. The front is a "Diablo" model measuring 4-3/4 inches wide and built for mid-glide front-end installation. Joe Appel

While the sleeker, more curvaceous Villain gas tank has proven to be Jesse James' most popular with aftermarket builders, we chose this simple but attractive West Coast Choppers King Sportster—or Peanut—tank. Just $250 retail, it's still packed with style from its flat gas cap with flush mounts to its flat bottom and Frisco-style mounting system. Joe Appel

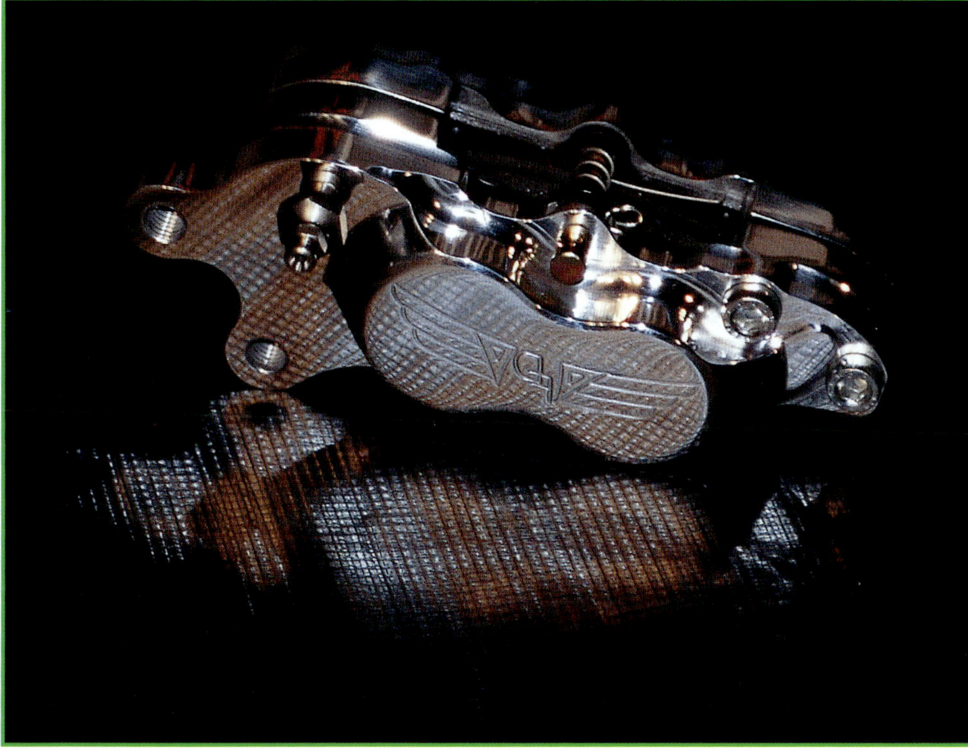

We'd decided to run a single brake on the front end to save a few bucks over the costs of a twin disc setup. This billet four-piston caliper from GMA should more than do the trick.

photos of other West Coast Choppers so we had a general idea of what the finished bike should look like, even at this early stage. Nearly every one had been outfitted with an open belt primary drive which runs cleaner and weighs considerably less than a greasy, maintenance-heavy, chain drive. Ours is a Primo 3-inch open belt drive that comes with a steel belt shroud to protect the odd pant leg or boot lace from becoming one with the transmission.

Picking and choosing the remaining parts followed a pre-chosen design, made easier because we already knew what we wanted in a finished product. There'll be no major headaches over whether to mount a passenger seat, sissy bar or pillion footrests if you make sure to have a clear idea of what your chopper will look like.

EL BRUTO POWER

But that still left us with the task of selecting an engine for our budget chop. There are literally dozens of

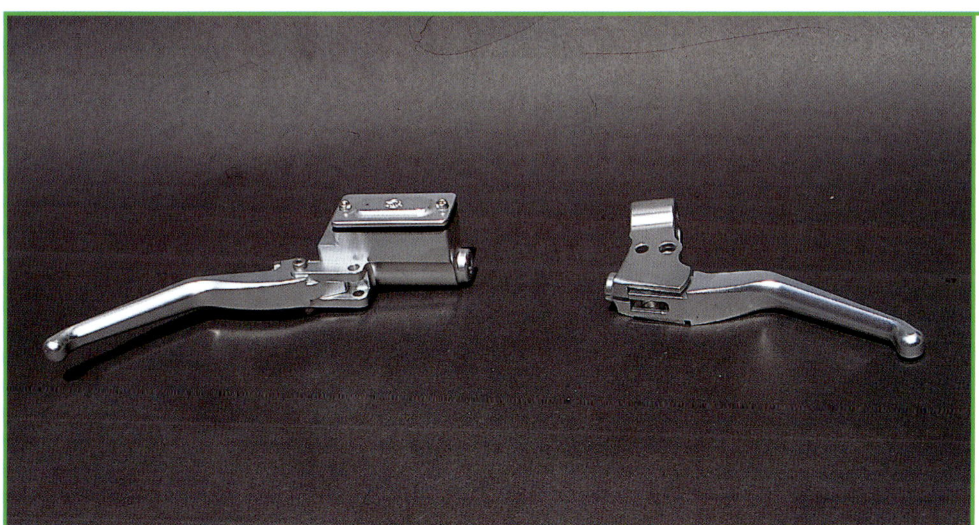

Matching clutch lever and 5/8-inch universal master cylinder both from GMA— these solid billet pieces were affordable (just $800 complete) and offer home customizers limitless options for powdercoating or color-anodizing. The simple clutch mount means we'll be running only a starter button, located on the oil tank.

With a massive powerplant, we were going to need some serious, stop-fast brakes to bring our chopper to a halt. This chromed, two-piston RST caliper includes a chromed mounting bracket and all billet aluminum construction for added strength.

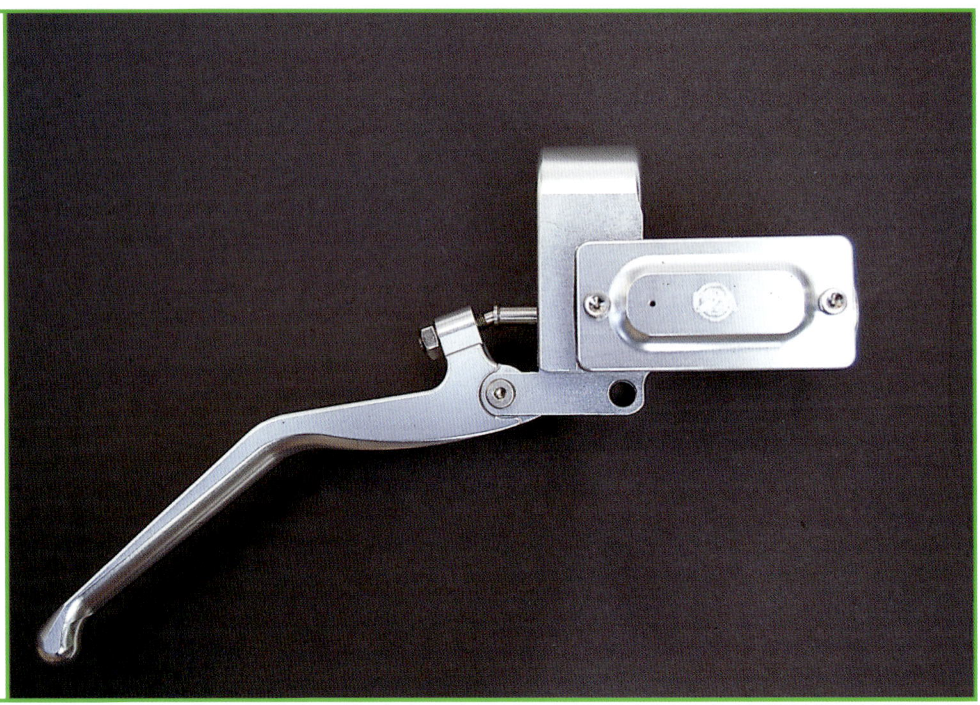

Detail of the GMA master cylinder, also available in chrome.

aftermarket V-twin motors being manufactured for custom applications today, with power characteristics ranging from those of stock Harleys to performance that could shame half the bikes at your local quarter-mile drag strip. The popular motto for chopper builders, both big names and average Joes alike, seems to be "Bigger is definitely better."

S&S has recently introduced a 145-cubic inch monster V-Twin and commissioned several renowned builders to create a motorcycle around it. Other big-inch engine manufacturers like Rev Tech and Patrick racing have developed a loyal following among celebrity chopper builders with their 120-cubic inch-plus engines, that easily pump out 120 horsepower and a staggering 100-plus foot-pounds of thudding torque.

Although a fire-breathing motor powerful enough

Sure, it's expensive at $499, but no West Coast Chopper is complete without the famed Maltese cross air cleaner. Jesse James also offers an Ace of Spades version through Custom Chrome, Inc.

Remember to create a checklist of necessary hard parts for your project chopper and try to keep them all in a single location. This Pingel fuel petcock is just the sort of easily misplaced but highly necessary item that will have builders tearing their hair out if it's gone.

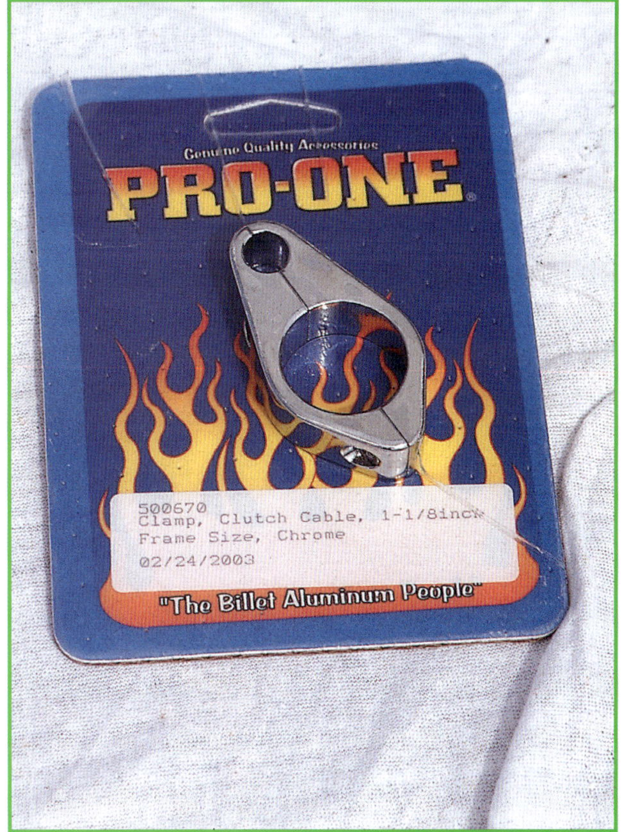

Hose and brake line clamps and guides will come in handy when routing your feed lines throughout your chopper. Lucky for us the Perse front forks have internal brake line routings in the triple clamps.

Brake lines can be cut by most custom motorcycle shops or catalog suppliers to fit any front fork length, but well-made stainless-steel versions like these Russell lines can be ordered to fit most custom applications. Braided lines not only look good, they offer more brake line pressure and faster stops.

A starter-shaft extension was necessary to clear the clutch plate on our Primo 3-inch open belt drive.

to propel a Humvee through city traffic may seem like the ultimate statement for a custom chopper, these larger engines carry with them some very specific maintenance requirements and can be a handful for riders unaccustomed to piloting choppers. One hundred twenty is a whole lotta horses, and when they're unleashed in a motorcycle with long forks and no rear suspension they can strain the skills of even the most experienced chopper riders. Though today's custom chopper frames are manufactured from tough chrome moly steel with thick tubing, they have been known to suffer fractures from the added vibration of these mega-powerplants—finding a fissure in a $4,000 motorcycle frame would be a disaster, whether you were parked in the driveway or tooling along at 70 miles per hour.

I've spoken with several chopper builders who have installed stock-displacement Harley-Davidson 80-cubic inch motors in their rigid choppers and many say they still enjoy a brisk, torquey ride. Stock Evolu-

tion engines can be had for as little as $3,500 in plain finish—about half the cost of a big-inch stroker mill from a top-name performance house.

We figured we'd split the difference by opting for a high-performance motor with a mildly stroked motor which would provide plenty of power for an, um, heavier rider, while not being in such a radical state of tune that it would require constant maintenance or shake loose the chrome bits and pieces on the rest of our chopper.

We'd heard nothing but good about the El Bruto engines from Midwest Motorcycle Supply and Midwest's resident engine guru Kenny Francis listened to our needs and sent us running in the direction of their 113-cubic inch version (though a teeth-rattling 127-model is also available). The Evolution-style El Bruto is perfect for our needs, which will include lots of boulevard profiling and some daily riding where low-down torque and reliability are top concerns. The El Bruto 113 is engineered by Midwest's in-house per-

DO'S AND DON'TS

DO: Place all of your parts in a single space, if possible, to keep inventory of what you've bought and what's still needed. Misplaced parts can cause serious holdups once construction has begun.

DO: Buy in bulk. Even the most costly chopper components are cheaper when you buy several major components at once. Aftermarket houses like Custom Chrome Incorporated offer reasonable prices, but don't be afraid to go directly to the source and call West Coast Choppers for a good deal.

DO: Sketch a detailed idea of what your West Coast Chopper should look like, the length of fork you desire, paint schemes, etc., to use as a reference when all the nuts and bolts are finally turned. Not an artist? Pay a friend or creative type who's handy with a pencil to do it for you. The ability to refer back to your original plan is invaluable during a build.

DON'T: Mix and match parts from different builders. If you want a Jesse James chopper, stick with his parts and his parts only. A lesser brand part may look good on your budget ledger, but there's nothing like the real thing.

DON'T: Attempt to outdo the masters. Plenty of backyard chopper builders subscribe to the belief that do-it-yourself means fabricating your own hard parts like fenders, seats, etc. That's fine if you're talented and experienced. If not, stick to simple bolt-togethers which will keep you from getting in over your head.

DON'T: Panic. What may look like a lot of work is actually little more than a full-scale model kit. And as with those scale models of our youth, a few hours here and there for a consistent period of time will start to yield results.

---

formance firm known as Ultima. With a 4-inch bore and a 4.25-inch stroke, its forged pistons make a compression rate of 10.2:1.

We were way impressed with the high-end list of internal components the El Bruto boasts, from its .625 lift cam to its Crane pushrods, billet oil pump and tapped blocks, and centrifugally cast cylinder wall liners. Machined on state-of-the-art CNC equipment, the El Bruto has 30 percent more cooling fins than an Evolution mill, which makes for far cooler running—a real necessity for a city rider like myself. The motor comes in either a plain finish, black, or fully polished—the latter catching our eye, naturally.

The pleasant surprise was the El Bruto's cost—a complete ready-to-install motor retails for $6,600, which is a bargain for a chromed and polished powerplant throbbing out 125 foot-pounds of juicy torque and 125 license-losing rear wheel horsepower. The Midwest powerplants breathe best through an S&S

"D" ($409) series carburetor, as Francis warned that anything smaller than this, the largest off-the-shelf breather from S&S, may fuel-starve the stroker engine at high revs. There was no charging system or starter included with the Ultima motor which had to be purchased separately from CCI. Their complete Motor Factory high-output charging system kit includes a Premium alternator and a rectifier/regulator for $319, while a stroker motor demands a high-output 2.4-kilowatt starter which we picked up for $484.

Keeping track of the money we've spent while storing all of our parts in a well-lit garage space allows us to quickly inventory what's been purchased and what's still needed to finish our budget dream bike. It's important to store as many of the parts in one clear, well-lit space as possible to ensure you know where everything is once the building process begins. And with our money well spent, we're just about ready for a quick preliminary bolt-up to see what our chopper looks like in the raw.

THE ORIGINAL GREEN MEANIE C.F.L.

When Jesse James built this bike in late 1999, it was one of the first Chopper For Life rigid frame bikes he'd ever constructed. At the time, even West Coast Choppers was still churning out custom motorcycles steeped in the fatbike look popular at the time: wide, five-gallon fatbob gas tanks, flat handlebars frequently riding on aftermarket Softail-style frames. Jesse has said that the C.F.L., with its moderate, 38-degree rake, short forks, and reasonably stout wheelbase was built "for the way I like to ride a motorcycle." That is, fast and very aggressively.

To that end, Jesse concentrated on making this little green bar-hopper as nimble as possible (for a chopper, that is) with a mid-glide front fork only four inches longer than stock and footpegs and controls mounted comfortably in the stock Harley-Davidson position. The flat track-style handlebars were borrowed from an 883 Sportster while the brakes at either end are serious four-piston models from longtime West Coast Choppers collaborator Performance Machine. Powered by a show-polished 113-cubic-inch S&S Super Sidewinder motor, the relatively lightweight machine could actually lift its front wheel under hard acceleration—a feat a longer, more stretched-out chopper could never achieve.

This was the first complete chopper frame to roll out of West Coast Choppers and has provided the basis for dozens of custom projects over the ensuing years. This machine runs a stock Harley-Davidson Sportster gas tank with a 2.25-gallon fuel capacity which looks almost too small for the stretched backbone of the rigid chassis—the C.F.L. built in this book uses a longer 3-gallon Sportster fuel cell that fills the frame's contours a bit more fully.

Many of the signature parts and acccssories that have come to characterize the West Coast Chopper look are evident on this prototype, from the .44-magnum handlebar risers to the cylindrical oil bag and battery box located beneath the hand-stitched seat.

The Ace of Spades air cleaner is another signature W.C.C. accessory that's available to home builders though the Maltese cross version has proven more popular with builders. Check out the C.F.L. logo etched into the oil tank and the cool, color-matched headlight bucket. Details like these are relatively inexpensive and can really make a custom chopper stand out from the crowd.

The C.F.L. kits available through Custom Chrome, Inc. can be built to mimic this motor-cycle with a few notable differences in detail—those black enameled organ exhaust pipes with the chromed spiderweb heat shield are one-offs, unfortunately, and Jesse has never made them available to customers. The green metalflake paint with orange and yellow flames makes a bold, original statement and the wire wheels add an air of 1960s authenticity seldom seen in the age of computer-designed billet aluminum wheels.

At-home builders will typically have a lot less cash to spend on their C.F.L.s so trick bits like the Exile Cycles combination sprocket/brake rotor are pure luxuries—as is the weird, Russian-made spool hub rear wheel. Since the C.F.L. was first launched, the popularity of custom choppers with far wider rear tires than this bike's 200-millimeter hoop have become all the rage among professional and amateur builders alike. And while tires measuring 240 and even 280 millimeters in width (or about 10 inches) are visually stunning and create an almost exaggerated rear end for a chopper, they seldom allow a motorcycle to handle as sharply or steer as easily as a moderate-width tire like the one seen here. It all depends on whether you plan to use your West Coast Chopper for cruising the boulevards or just bar-hopping and collecting trophies on the show circuit—either way, it's gonna look cool.

CHAPTER 2
CREATING A ROLLING CHASSIS

Even for the master custom motorcycle craftsmen around the world, each chopper that rolls out of their garages must be built not one, but two complete times before it's considered finished. Tell this to the average layman, and they'll likely think they've just met the world's most obsessive-compulsive bike rider, some wrench-happy nut who gets his jollies spending long nights in greasy garages instead of cruising the boulevards. But the process of first constructing a raw unpainted rolling chassis from your chopper kit is not only a necessity; it's a step that, if overlooked, would make the completed motorcycle far less rideable.

Previous and this page: Before we could begin constructing a rolling chassis out of our West Coast Chopper parts, we had to perform a little quick fix-it. The rear Two-Eight fender didn't line up perfectly with the hidden mounts on the rear hardtail section of our chassis, so out came the grinder. The mounts had to be angled on the frame's right side and then re-tapped with new threads. That done, the fender was remounted with a perfectly square alignment. Steven Dietz

The bare chassis (painted black with primer to aid workshop visuals—the real primer and paint will be covered extensively in Chapter IV) is inspected for any irregularities. Steve Peffer, our ace builder, will re-tap any mounting holes with sloppy threads. Steven Dietz

Above and opposite: The rear fender bolts to the frame courtesy of our $1/2$-inch bolts on the inside of the fender. Make sure it doesn't appear to lean toward one side or another. Steven Dietz

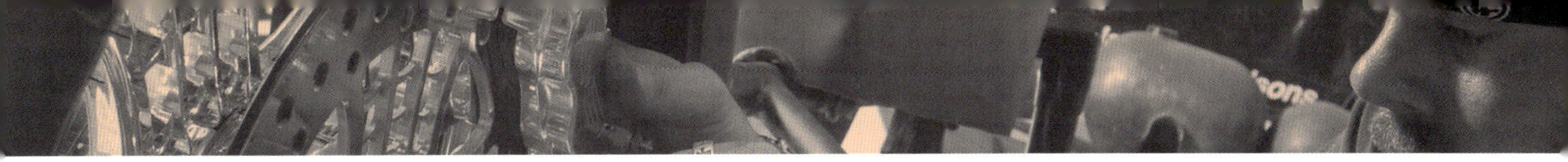

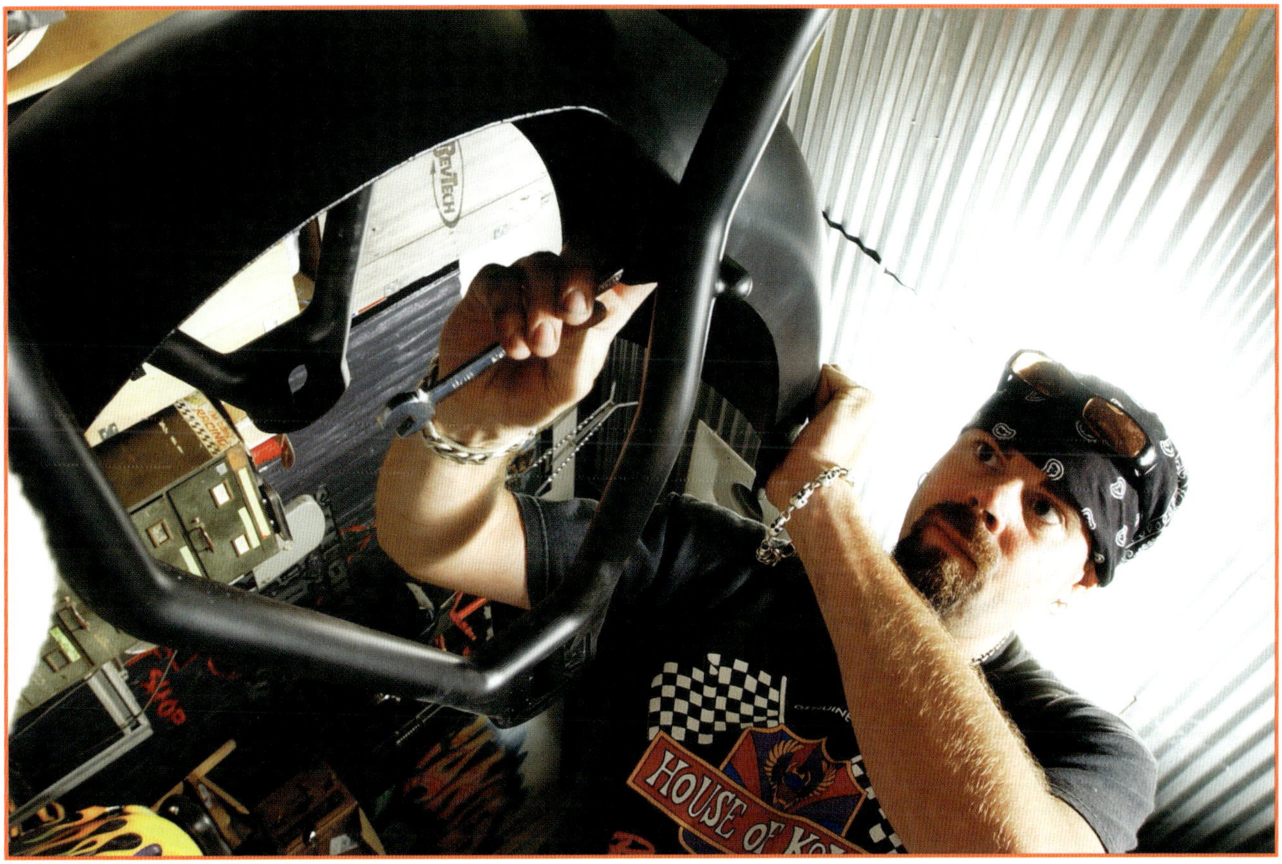

HOUSE OF KOLOR
Racing Team

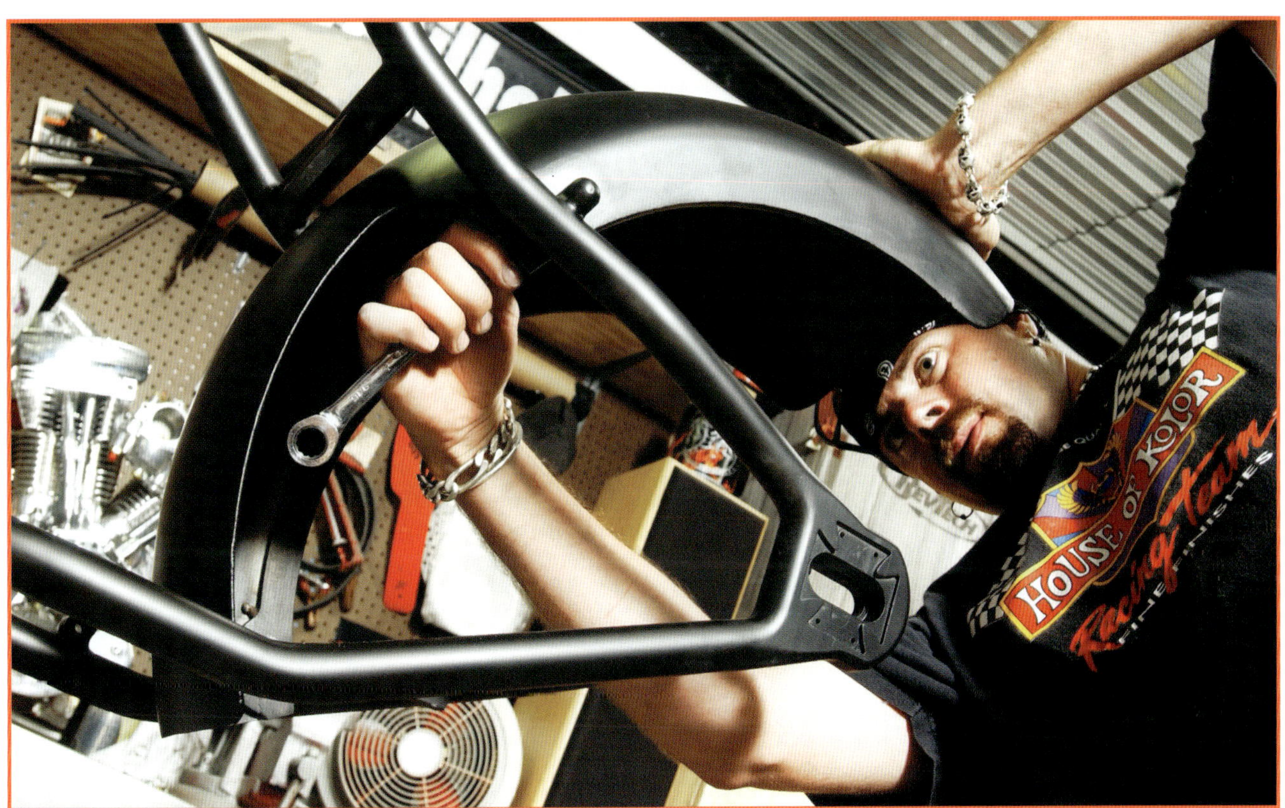

Moving towards the front of the motorcycle, Steve inserts the bearings into the frame neck. The internal fork stops require four small holes be drilled in the neck and a series of four stopper pins inserted. Steven Dietz *Opposite: The Perse front forks are mounted on the chassis by lifting them from below the chassis as it rests on the lift stand.* Steven Dietz

The best way to understand the usefulness of a rolling chassis chopper to is take a walk back down memory lane to those Revell or Monogram model car kits we built as kids. In the illustrated instruction booklets, scale modelers were instructed to do two things without fail: One was to avoid sniffing the highly toxic glue (and some of us didn't listen, did we?), and the other involved pre-fitting each of the adjoining plastic parts together before any glue had been applied. This step allowed us to see whether *bumper A* would adjoin seamlessly with *rear quarter panel C.* Looking back, it's obvious that a perfunctory fitting-together of our model kit's parts saved us from the potential construction mishaps had we simply smeared the plastic bits with glue and forged ahead.

Despite the exacting work of engineers and designers, even the most detailed model kits could end up requiring the services of an X-Acto knife when parts didn't fit together as planned.

It's not much different when it comes to constructing a West Coast Chopper—or any other kit bike for that matter—from parts. A mockup build allows us to fix what needs fixin' and correct mechanical imperfections before some of the heavier and more complex mechanicals, like drivetrain components, electrical parts, and the tough-to-mount engine are in place. You'll want to see whether the profile of your dream chopper matches the sketches and photos you've studied (remember those?), or if you want to exchange any major part,

Above and opposite: With the Weld front wheel and tire already attached, the fork is maneuvered into place. The fork's hex-shaped sliders are loosened and slid downward so the top triple clamp can be removed in order to slide the fork stem through the neck bearings. Steven Dietz

Using a torque wrench, the bottom nut is tightened—Perse forks don't utilize a top nut due to their smoothed top triple clamp.
Steven Dietz

With the bottom clamp secured, the hexed slider can be wound back towards the top triple clamp. Be sure to tighten the twin pinch bolts located on the sides of the bottom clamp.
Steven Dietz

Ancillary items including the oil tank/battery box are attached using a T-handle driver and hex-head bolts. Make sure to use lock washers on these metal-on-metal mountings. Steven Dietz

Next, mount the gas tank using the front mounting bolt through the frame. Steve checks to make sure the holes beneath the tank line up with the twin mounting straps he'll bolt on next. Steven Dietz

The gas tank mounted, it's finally starting to look something like a chopper. If—and only if—you're finished for the day, kick back with your favorite malt beverage and check out your progress. Nice! Steven Dietz

like a fender, gas tank, wheel, or even a frame before going any further with your project. How about comfort? Does the amount of rake in your frame make the front end feel balanced and easy to steer, or does it flop from side to side when the handlebars are turned? And as for those handlebars, the rolling chassis phase permits a builder to experiment with several widths, heights, and designs and also determine whether the bars and risers will easily clear the gas tank once installed.

This is also a good time to arrange the workspace you'll be using to construct your own West Coast Chopper. We were fortunate enough to have the small, but well-appointed, workshop of Steve Peffer, owner of Steel City Choppers, at our disposal. This meant that unlike, say, building the chopper in a home garage, we wouldn't have to move the bike from the lift when it was needed for some other purpose or move our parts stash when it came time to roll out the lawnmower. It's in your best interest to find a clean, roomy, and

Big Bob Miller hoists the rear wheel onto the workbench to slide it between the frame rails; after sliding the rear axle through the hub, be sure to check for clearance around the wheel and fender—you'll want to sort out any points of contact between these parts now, before painting the motorcycle. Steven Dietz

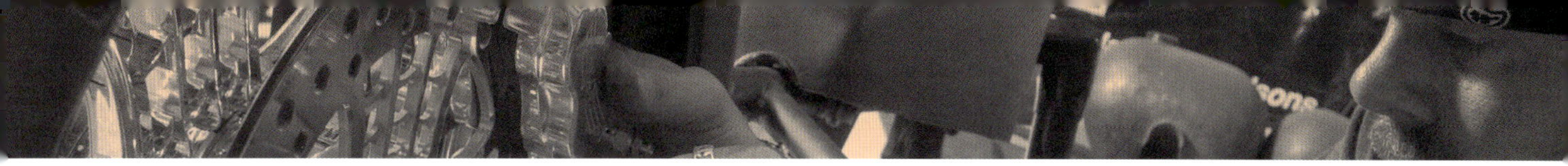

With the brake rotor bolted to the wheel hub, Steve threads the rear axle through the brake caliper mounting arm. With the RST caliper in place on the mounting arm, the wheel should turn freely without disturbing the caliper. Steven Dietz

Next come the West Coast Choppers handlebar risers which Steve will mount . . . Steven Dietz

. . . through the two holes in the top triple clamp. The fastening nuts should be tightened fairly securely (right) as the handlebars will be used to roll the chassis around during this phase of construction. Steven Dietz

Remove those cool-looking .44-magnum end caps by unthreading them counterclockwise to install the handlebars. Steven Dietz

This is a good time to experiment with several different types of handlebars: these Z-bars offer a short reach to the front end, but we also checked out a set of flat drag-style bars and a pair of flat-track-style bars from an 883 Sportster. Arm length, height, and seating position can all affect your handlebar choice. Steven Dietz

extremely well lit and well ventilated space to build your chopper—a place where your work in progress will not be interfered with or disturbed in any way.

If your garage has room for it, a professional quality shop lift stand, as used by the service departments in most all motorcycle dealerships, is a great buy as it places the motorcycle at a comfortable, chest-high level making it easier to work on. Manual versions can be had for about $350 and air-assisted lifts for about twice that—not cheap, but they'll definitely pay for themselves considering the lower back pain you'd get from wrenching together a chopper bent over on the floor!

Because we've set out to make this at-home chopper project as easy for an average shade tree mechanic as possible, our chopper requires very little or no welding and little parts fabrication. We're focusing on simple bolt-up construction, which is what the rolling chassis is now ready for. An electric power drill is a necessity, as is a ruler for measuring and a non-permanent marker (or wax pencil) for marking clearances. A couple of solid, 4 x 4 wooden blocks about 18 inches long are a must-have for propping up the frame on your lift stand when the wheels are removed. You'll also need a good set of mechanic's wrenches, both ratchets and open-end and box versions; a standard-sized rubber mallet for pounding axles through; some T-handle hex drivers in standard sizes; screwdrivers, both Phillips and slotted; a standard set of taps and dies to ensure there's no faulty mounting holes in parts or frames are a good choice, as is the addition of

Unless you plan to try out for a spot on the U.S. Olympic Hernia Team, we suggest enlisting help when mounting the engine. Some chopper builders prefer to pay the frame down sideways over the motor; Steve and shop mechanic Jared Steithner do it the hard way. Steven Dietz

a long-handled torque wrench for securing axles, forks, and other driveline parts.

CLASSY CHASSIS

Keeping in mind that even the wildest kit bike is really nothing more than a giant scale model kit for grown-ups, we approached our rolling chassis determined to have fun. And why not—at this point, we'd get an early look at how the parts we'd purchased would finally look all bolted together, which is something most chopper builders are more than eager to do.

The Perse front forks came complete and fully assembled from the manufacturer, but because they will be the first major component to be mated to the rolling chassis mockup, they'll require a partial tear-down to install. Steve first loosened the side hex nuts on the lower triple clamp that secure the fork tubes to the assembly before loosening the large bottom nut from its recessed position beneath the bottom triple clamp and loosened the hex-shaped sliders on each fork tube before using a rubber mallet to gently force the upper fork assembly downward. He removed the fork bearings from the front-end assembly, installing them into the frame neck before sliding the lower triple tree into place and securing it with the aforementioned bottom nut. Through the bottom triple clamp holes come the fork tubes (greased lightly to ensure smooth re-installation); they're fed into place and the top triple clamp secured with the fork sliders snugged back into place. Perse's instruction kit details

The transmission bolts in fairly easily from the right side of the motorcycle. The mounting holes in the frame must be accessed from underneath the chassis. Steven Dietz

You may want to remove the gas tank before mounting the engine as it blocks access to the top boxed motor mount. Steven Dietz

Have an assistant help jiggle the engine in the frame if you're having difficulty reaching the motor mounting bolts properly. Pinched fingers are no fun! Steven Dietz

The Primo belt drive unit can now be installed on the left side. Make sure the transmission's starter shaft clears the clutch backing plate which secures with eight long Allen bolts. Steven Dietz

Next up is the belt drive's primary backing plate. The main engine shaft slides through the main port while Allen-head bolts again lock the unit into place. Steven Dietz

Our CCI kickstand is test-bolted into place to make sure it will align properly with the primary belt once it's installed on the twin pulleys. When ordering your kickstand, make sure to specify the rake and fork extension of your chopper as a too-long kickstand can interfere with belt operation. Steven Dietz

The clutch basket and rear pulley installed over the transmission main shaft. The rear drive chain's sprocket is installed on the shaft first and is hidden from view by the clutch in this photo. After fitting the drive pulley in front, slip the Kevlar belt over both pulleys before tightening them. Steven Dietz

torque specs for tightening the lateral pinch bolts that keep the tubes from turning, used because his forks do not utilize a top bolt as most others do. We also needed to drill four small holes into the frame to accommodate the C.F.L.'s internal fork stops. These small holes allowed the insertion of four set pins that we tapped in with a small hammer just beneath the dust shields at the top and bottom of the neck.

We then picked up our 3-gallon Sportster-style gas tank, positioning it on the frame along the carefully positioned mounting holes. When we ordered the C.F.L. frame, the folks at CCI asked us to specify whether we were using a Sportster tank or one of West Coast's stretched Villain units. The chassis arrived with pre-welded threaded mounts for whichever tank is specified, making mounting a simple affair of bolting the four bottom-mounting bolts and the single front bolt into place.

The tank goes on before the next piece, the 8-inch Jesse James handlebar risers with the .44-magnum top caps. This way, we're able to ascertain whether the motorcycle's frame rake coexists peacefully with the angle of the flush-mounted (or Friscoed) gas tank. Too often, chopper builders will construct a bike with a lazy rake angle of 40 degrees or more, only to find the 12-inch handlebar risers will bang clumsily into the top of the gas tank. With clearance assured, we make a note to later try on several different pairs of handle-

Now the belt drive's backing plates can be secured. Steven Dietz

bars to find which riding posture best suits our style, the motorcycle, and, of course, our lower backs!

Moving around to the rear of the chassis which is still resting atop those two wooden support blocks, Steve gets started mounting the rear Weld Widow wheel. We started by first placing the bare metal C.F.L. rigid frame onto the shop lift. The Maltese cross rear axle covers can be removed with a pair of small Phillips screws on both sides, and we carefully placed them in a plastic Tupperware bowl for safe-keeping. From there, the rear axle slides out and the rear wheel, complete with matching chromed 13-inch brake rotor, is slid into place. The axle is then re-inserted with assistance from a rubber mallet. Next comes the 9-inch-wide, Two-Eight Jesse James fender.

Designed to be affixed to the frame via a set of very clever hidden mounts (they resemble bullets and are welded to the rear hardtail), the fender should prove a breeze to bolt in place.

But one of the fender mounts turns out to have been incorrectly aligned, throwing the rear end terribly out of shape. With the rear wheel and its 200-mm tire in place, the right side of the fender, when bolted in place, sags uncomfortably into the rubber sidewall, preventing the wheel assembly from turning freely. Instances like this are precisely why rolling chassis mock-ups are such a necessity, and it allows Steve to figure out a quick fix to the fender alignment problem. He ends up aligning the fender to three of the four mounts, choosing to use a wax pencil to mark the

ERRATA

How to Build a West Coast Choppers Kit Bike

First published in September, 2004

Please note the following changes which were found once the book was first printed but not yet released. Motorbooks International's goal is to publish the most accurate information we can. We recognize that some words, model names, and designations, for example, mentioned herein are the property of the trademark holders. We use them for identification purposes only.

THIS BOOK IS NOT AN OFFICIALLY LICENSED PUBLICATION OF WEST COAST CHOPPERS.

Page 8, top photo caption: The wheel rims on the motorcycle depicted are painted rather than powder coated. The dual exhausts are LBC not Cordova.

Bottom photo caption: The gas tank is correctly a one-off West Coast Choppers custom (not for sale) and the gas cap was not designed by West Coast Choppers.

Page 9: The custom-only *El Diablo II* depicted in the photograph does not use a Softail-type frame but rather has a rigid frame.

Page 10, bottom photo caption: West Coast Choppers offers Z-shaped handlebars as a custom option only; they are not for retail sale.

Page 11: The motorcycle depicted is a one-off, custom *El Diablo* and is not built from a C.F.L. kit and thus the stated dimensions are not applicable.

Page 12: The motorcycle depicted is owned by Ron Ianotti, and not Tom Ianotti. Moreover, the *El Diablo* is not a lowrider, was not built during the winter of 1999, and does not use the Dragon Softail frame.

Page 16: The *El Diablo* does not use a Dragon Softail frame. West Coast Choppers no longer manufactures the Dragon frame.

Page 33: The motorcycle depicted uses the first "commissioned" frame and not the first "complete" frame.

While Steve was busy with the belt drive Bob and Jared affixed the left side Ness Radius forward control unit. A chrome shift rod was then affixed to the shifter arm and the transmission linkage. Steven Dietz

With the gas tank removed for an unobstructed view of the engine, we get a feel for how the massive 113-cubic-inch Midwest El Bruto looks in its home. Additional clearance above the rocker boxes means an even taller, larger displacement motor could have been used. Steven Dietz

spot on the fender where the mount would line up if it hadn't been slightly off-center. Drilling a new mounting port into the fender, Steve will later putty over the extra hole when applying filler putty to the bodywork in Chapter 3. While re-mounting the wheel and fender, we check for clearance between the tire sidewalls (you should ideally hope for about ⅛ inch on both sides to allow for heat expansion) and we slide the PFM brake caliper mounting arm over the axle making sure it clears the rotor and rolls freely with the rear wheel.

Moving back toward the front of the bike, we pause at the engine bay and start bolting on the ancillary equipment. The cylindrical West Coast Choppers chrome oil tank bolts easily into place, via a quartet of ½-inch bolts, with the integral battery box slotting in neatly in the space below where the set pan will eventually fit.

As we won't be bothering with connecting the oil lines or electrical wiring at this point, we can quickly continue with our assembly, next installing the 5-speed Twin Power transmission. Be careful not to smash your digits with this job, as this baby is no lightweight. Lucky for us, the polished-case gearbox has been well designed and slots easily into place atop the flat transmission mount on the frame. A set of four massive ($1\frac{1}{16}$-inch) bolts hold the transmission in place and can be attached by reaching beneath the chassis (thanks to those wooden blocks again) for access.

Though several different techniques exist to mount a big-inch V-twin engine into a frame, from laying the engine down flat on the workbench and dropping the frame over it, to rolling the motor into a standing frame using specially-made Harley-Davidson wheeled jigs, the most common (and dramatic) method involves simply lifting the 150-pound lump in one's arms and walking it into place. We've all seen this done in countless Discovery Channel TV shows and in the pages of biker magazines, but a word of warning is prudent here: If you've got a weak back, or are less than familiar with mounting motors, we suggest getting a little help before tackling this job the way we did. Steve Peffer has installed dozens of V-twin powerplants this way so he had no problems hooking up our Ultima powerplant. You may not be so lucky. However you get the engine shoved into its place in the frame, this is a good time to familiarize yourself with the various mounting points that will secure the motor to its chassis. Because we aren't yet assembling the top motor mount that attaches the top end to the boxed motor mount beneath the gas tank, we fasten the four heavy bolts in the front lat-

The front Hell Bent exhaust pipe fastens to the engine head via an internal threaded hole. Because all the parts are genuine West Coast Choppers, there won't be any guesswork when it comes to fittings—in many cases, radically bent exhaust pipes will fail to clear frame rails. Steven Dietz

A special "L" shaped exhaust bracket was sourced from CCI to affix the rear Hell Bent pipe to the frame. Nifty lower mounting holes mean no fabricating brackets. Steven Dietz

eral motor mount (they'll eventually be torqued to 25 foot-pounds) and the two rear top bolts located near the transmission case.

We attach the S&S "D" series carburetor to the manifold, affixing the four retaining bolts that hold the West Coast Choppers Maltese cross air cleaner into place on the engine's right side and, using an "L"-shaped lower mount, the Hell Bent exhaust pipes are grafted onto the engine, giving the engine compartment that "strictly business" appearance so associated with Jesse James choppers.

Stepping back for a look, the motorcycle is definitely beginning to take shape. In little more than two eight-hour days of labor, we're already reaching that phase in the build where that huge box of parts that's been taking up so much valuable floor space in the garage looks and feels like an actual motorcycle. And not just any motorcycle, but a genuine West Coast Chopper.

We move back to the front end, removing the hidden axle covers with a set of tiny Allen screws (remem-ber that Tupperware bowl again) to slide the wheel shaft out. Lubricating the axle lightly with a little spray-on lubricant, we install the front Weld Widow wheel with attached brake rotor. The front fender is then placed, not bolted, inside the fork's lower legs to measure how well it fits. We'd had the foresight to order a pair of spacers from West Coast's parts department along with the front fender which, it turns out, we'll need. It's a valuable lesson in what fits what—most chopper parts builders manufacture fenders to fit the diameter of a particular wheel they're using in a custom application and whether that fender is a perfect match with any of the myriad front ends on the market can be a hit-or-miss proposition. The Perse front end is of a standard Wide Glide width, which means the Jesse James fender will fit with the use of our spacers, but once in place there's enough clearance in between the 21 x 2.15 Metzeler tire to allow for the expansion that occurs when tires are heated up from road use.

Bad, mad, and all decked out in more flat black than the crowd at a Goth concert, our rolling chassis version of a West Coast Chopper looks almost too good to paint. Many viewers suggested we leave it this way. Steven Dietz

DO'S AND DON'TS

DO: Step back and look at your chopper as the mockup build progresses. This is the perfect time to switch any major components that don't look right or fit your body or riding style.

DO: Carefully inspect each part before bolting it on—even the best-made parts occasionally have manufacturing defects. Re-tap any threaded holes that may need fresh threading.

DO: Using a floor jack, spin each wheel to ensure the brake calipers are separating above the rotors smoothly and cleanly. There should be about $\frac{1}{8}$-inch clearance between each side of the fenders and tires to allow the tires to expand as they will at road speeds.

DON'T: Bother installing any electrical wiring at this stage, but try a mock fitting of your major electrical components like the rectifier, voltage regulator, etc. Drill any holes now, before the chassis is painted.

DON'T: Forget to check and re-check your written parts list—anything that's missing needs to be bolted on now.

DON'T: Be afraid to call your parts distributor if something doesn't fit—most times, they'll replace a defective part for free.

It's a good idea to stop and take photos of your chopper during different stages of its construction. Joe Appel

Next come the Primo belt-drive clutch plates, which are bolted to the transmission after threading the mainshaft through the chromed plate. The front engine plate of the belt drive is then bolted into place with a set of long Allen bolts that affix the unit to the transmission. The 3-inch Kevlar belt is stretched over the twin belt pulleys that are then slipped over the engine shaft and the transmission shaft. We won't bother adjusting either for tension at this stage as we're going to reassemble the motor and drivetrain shortly.

The Ness Radius forward controls are mounted to their posts on each side of the forward motor mounts. Due to their unique design that incorporates the rear master cylinder within the controls, these footpegs must be first disassembled before they can be attached to the motorcycle. This involves removing the brake pedal

With the sheet metal parts in place, take a good, long look at your progress. Are the fenders shaped to your liking? Does the gas tank fill the frame top rail fully? If not, this is the time to make changes. *Joe Appel*

from the assembly before mounting the controls (and much the same for the shifter side control) and detaching a small wave spring unit, all of which is covered in detail within the individual Ness instruction booklet.

By bolting the footpegs into place, we're able to test-seat the motorcycle to see whether she fits our personal riding style. This is the best time to experiment with all sorts of ancillaries like rearview mirrors (which few truly bad-assed choppers bother with!) handlebar height and width, etc., because from here we're going to strip down the entire rolling chassis and ship the sheet metal and chassis off for a stint of body molding and a visit to the spray-paint booth, otherwise known as the point of no return!

STONE'S CUSTOM CYCLES

To ward off thieves and overzealous tourists, the owner chained this bike to a telephone pole in Daytona Beach. At a rally overrun with chrome-laden bikes that pack all the subtlety of Mr. T's jewelry collection, this homemade Jesse James-style hardtail chopper is a classy and rare example of subtle custom styling. The single-color metalflake blue paint job is unusual for a rigid West Coast Chopper, bikes that typically find themselves splashed with wild flame jobs or colors right out of a pack of Skittles candy. Still, this chopper has its own share of fetching eye-candy, from the Dakota digital speedometer that's been cut into the 3-gallon West Coast Choppers Villain gas tank to the chromed wire wheels front and rear. Instead of overdosing on chrome plating, this owner opted to treat his handlebar risers and air cleaner to a coating of black anodizing, an affordable, durable finish that requires far less maintenance than chrome. The rigid frame is actually of unknown origin, though resembling the West Coast C.F.L. in rake, design, and overall appearance. By adding one of W.C.C.'s Ace of Spades air cleaners, it has taken on the look of a C.F.L. for perhaps a fraction of the cost.

Though this machine has clearly been built to attract attention, several of the major components reveal it was completed on a realistic budget. The wire wheels are far cheaper options than any of the CNC machined billet rims currently on the market and the taillight/license plate holder is likely a swap meet special. The job of wiring this chopper was made easier for the builder by utilizing the stock Harley-Davidson handlebar switchgear, eliminating the need for custom controls and special wiring modifications. The stock cushioned-rubber handgrips are also still in use on this machine, the rider likely tiring of the blisters accrued from riding choppers with the fashionable, but grueling, knurled aluminum handgrips. That's an off-the-rack LePera solo seat and a final belt drive that might have started its life aboard a Springer Softail. The original spiderweb frame gusset has been replaced by a smaller, flame-design support while the front forks appear to be stock Harley Wide Glide items with shaved and chromed lower legs and even the stock fender pressed into chopper duty to save a few bucks.

A chopper like this, with its street-legal rearview mirrors and speedometer, will attract far less attention from the local constabulary than a machine built to flaunt inspection laws, but those choices are as individual as the owners.

CHAPTER 3

PREPPING FOR PAINT, BODYWORK, AND PRIMERS

Even though those boxes full of shapely, cool-looking sheet metal parts from West Coast Choppers may arrive at your door looking fit enough to simply bolt together to create a chopper, they're not quite finished. If you're like most novice motorcycle builders, you probably imagined a coat of primer would be enough to ready any motorcycle part for painting, but our expert chopper craftsman Steve Peffer, enlisted from his work at Steel City Choppers outside Pittsburgh, knows otherwise.

New motorcycle gas tanks, fenders, and even frames leave a manufacturer's warehouse with a rela-tively smooth finish as a result of several passes with an electric handheld grinder. But these bare metal surfaces are far from ready for painting, Steve explained. Before the first pass of an air gun can cross their surfaces, rough welds like those found on the gas tanks and fenders must be ground off with an electric grinder or smooth-covered in some sort of finishing material. By finishing material, we mean one of the many fiberglass-based resins that can be applied to gas tanks, frames, and fenders in order to smooth out any surface irregularities, welding seams, or imperfections that still remain.

Using a simple flat of cardboard with a dollop of Bondo fiberglass-based body putty, Steve works his way along the chassis applying the material to any welds or exposed seams.

Before beginning his body putty session, Steve carefully cleans the entire surface of the chassis with Acryli-Clean, a synthetic grease and wax remover. Residue from shipping or construction can prevent Bondo, primer, and paint from adhering to metal surfaces.

This is, unfortunately, one of the better-kept secrets in all of chopperdom and, I suspect, why so many unfinished kit bikes can be found for sale in newspapers and on the Internet auction house eBay. A visit to a bodyshop and then a qualified professional custom painter can easily add several thousand dollars to the construction costs of a kit bike, an expense many at-home builders forget to factor in when planning their dream rides. Fortunately, bodywork is not an exact science, and home builders willing to experiment may find themselves better qualified to perform this necessary step themselves.

If you're willing to have a go—and our expert builder Peffer claims anyone with patience and the ability to read instructions can do so—try practicing your Bondo skills on an old discarded fender or the quarter panel of a car before slapping a putty knife on your expensive new chopper parts. After a few tries at the following steps you still don't feel confident of your abilities to create a smooth surface on a piece of sheet metal, don't be ashamed—that's what auto body shops are for and most will be willing to help out by having one of their guys perform the paint prep work for you.

This can be an arduous, tedious, and exacting part of preparing your homemade chopper for the spray booth, but it must be performed prior to our next step, which involves painting the motorcycle. But before we get ahead of ourselves with the business of applying color to our chopper, let's head over to the body shop to see just how well we do with a jar of fiberglass and a putty knife.

PUTTY IN OUR HANDS

Steve Peffer has built dozens of custom choppers over the last decade or so and says he's occasionally done so without prepping the sheet metal parts with body filler, though when the motorcycle is painted and rolled onto the streets, the finish always seems to lack a certain smoothness. So to ensure show-level finishes on his choppers, Peffer always lays on a coat of Bondo

Though experienced body men like Steve can work wonders applying Bondo with bare fingers, we suggest using a small putty knife or applicator.

Several coats of putty may be necessary to smooth out some of the rougher welds and grind marks left on new chopper parts—here Steve uses medium-grit sandpaper to smooth over work he's just finished.

fiberglass body filler compound, which is a heavy and flexible body putty manufactured specifically to mask out welding marks and other surface imperfections—sort of like the Estee Lauder base makeup our wives and girlfriends use to cover their own imperfections. And just like make-up, it may take a few attempts to understand how best to apply a smooth and, more important, unnoticeable coat of Bondo putty before getting it right.

Following the detailed instructions on the package, the compound is mixed into a water solution and stirred until a consistency somewhere on the far side of creamy peanut butter is achieved. This stuff hardens faster than a divorcee's heart, so be careful to keep a pitcher of water nearby to loosen the mixture when necessary. Make sure you've first used a sandblasting cabinet to remove any oil or dirt remaining on the parts from their manufacture, which should be done with the finest-grit sand available. If you don't have access to a sandblasting cabinet (which most motor-

cycle shops have and will let you use for a brief time) try wiping down the sheet metal parts with a clean cloth and some Acrily-Clean wax and grease-removal solution. In an emergency, even a decent dishwashing liquid will suffice for removing any surface grease or dirt, which the filler compound will refuse to adhere to. But make sure to thoroughly dry all the parts before moving on to the next step, and use compressed air (available either through a compressor and hose setup or in cheap canned versions) to make sure the parts are totally clean.

Using a body spreader (which is a piece of flat, smooth plastic cut to about 4 x 4 inches and available for a few bucks at any auto parts store) dip into the Bondo and slowly spread it to cover the complete surfaces of the sheet metal parts, working along the broader surfaces first. It's OK to be a little sloppy here as excess material can be trimmed off with a wet sponge but be sure to do so before this goop starts to harden.

69

Any surfaces of your chopper that will be easily visible to the viewing public need to be smoother than a night club pick-up line; don't rush through the bodywork and you'll be rewarded with a mirror finish after the bike's been painted.

Steve plugged the mounting holes with small dowels made from rolled-up cardboard while applying putty to the fenders, and strongly suggests taping off the fuel filler port in the gas tank as well. The goal here is to apply an even coat to all surfaces without altering the contours of your parts—admittedly, this is one of the hardest steps in building your West Coast Chopper and no one could blame you for enlisting professional help with this segment of the construction process. A trained and experienced body man will have far more success with this exacting and time-consuming work than us raw amateurs. However, if you're the dyed-in-the-steel-wool DIY type, self-prepping your sheet metal parts can be greatly rewarding and provides a valuable skill you can use again when building choppers in the future.

All said, this may take some trial and a few errors. But Steve says those who are patient, diligent, and

Steve applies Bondo over the open channel along the frame's backbone, but he'll later need to drill this section out to route the electrical wiring harness.

willing to possibly practice on an old, discarded fender or two will achieve passable results in time.

Working in your favor is the fact that the parts will not require perfectly smooth surfaces at this point as you're basically laying down a coat of material that's dense enough to hide the blemishes, welds, and rough swirls left behind by steel-finishing equipment. That's what the next coat, known as filler primer, is for. After allowing enough time for the Bondo to properly cure (details, again, are in the packaged instructions) Steve suggests a quick surface sanding with 80-grit sandpaper to smooth out the rougher edges and excess material that may be hanging from parts edges. Again using compressed air to blow the surfaces clean of dust and particles of Bondo, you can use your hand to glide across the surface of your tank and fenders to feel whether there's any major unevenness or divots in the bodywork. If something feels terribly wrong, like

there's a rise on the top of a fender that wasn't there before, that's OK—bodywork is a famously forgiving and inexact science. Using a small, handheld electric grinder or sandpaper, mistakes and uneven surfaces can be smoothed out and the Bondo re-applied if necessary. We found the rough welds along the front tunnel on the West Coast Choppers Sportster-style gas tank to be a particularly difficult section to mold over, the rippled weld edges requiring several passes with a hand grinder and some rough 80-grit emery paper before it was even close to being level enough for molding. For these extremely rough sections, Steve applied a heavier compound known as Duraglass, which filled in the gaps nicely in a couple of coats. Besides that, few other areas on the sheet metal required a great deal of preparation work.

That done, start mixing the second finishing coat. This time we chose a lightweight body filler known as

When you can run your hands around frame rail junctions and over seams without feeling any catch or resistance from the surfaces, you've pretty much achieved Bondo nirvana; make sure to blow any dust or residue away with compressed air before parking these babies in the paint booth.

Evercoat that's far less dense and easier to spread than the first coat. This is also a compound that could be easily applied with a body spreader using flowing, back-to-front motions. This will be a far thinner coat than the previous Bondo coat and your aim here is to create a surface that's smooth enough to look good when painted, but still porous enough to absorb the initial primer coats as paint will not stick to a glass-smooth surface.

To this end, wait for the Evercoat to dry (which doesn't take long, as this is what's known as a high-solids primer) before starting the extensive wet-sanding process. Using extremely fine 600-grit sandpaper, keep the body parts surfaces wet with a bucket of cool water kept nearby, while gently smoothing over the surfaces for the better part of four hours—or until the parts yield a surface that feels uniform and seamless to the touch. Don't be afraid to show your progress to friends who've performed similar work on their own motorcycles. Soliciting advice on the progress you're making never hurt anyone. And remember to use a sanding block—that is, a small block of wood that comfortably fits into the center of your hand and wrapped in medium-grit sandpaper—to flatten all the edges along the underside of the gas tank and the edges of your fenders.

A sanding drum on a Dremmel or similar high-speed rotary tool can be used to clean away any buildup that may have collected in bolt holes and along mounting points. A Dremmel tool can also be utilized to shore up the rounded contours along the underside of the front fender which must appear razor-sharp when finished. Any of the Dremmel's tubular sanding wheels can be used for this purpose or, if you prefer, a piece of wooden dowel rod wrapped in sandpaper for wet-sanding applications. Though you'll need to remove the flush-mount gas cap during this step, it's best to close the open gas filler hole with masking tape to help prevent any putty from getting inside the tank.

And be prepared to mix another batch of Evercoat for the welding seams on your C.F.L. chassis, which

Close-up detailing of the spiderweb frame gusset on our Jesse James chassis after receiving a coat of Bondo—even the tiniest details can be improved with a little putty.

The bare metal covered in a light and even coat of Bondo, any surface irregularities have been masked for painting. Steven Dietz

Time-consuming and tedious, several coats of body filler must be applied to the bare sheet metal parts. In between each coat, wet sand the surface with 400-grit paper until a glasslike surface is achieved. Steven Dietz

The roughest welds on our entire chopper project were left around the Sportster gas tank's front end; Steve spent the better part of eight hours at work on this area. First came a session with a high-speed grinder to remove leftover weld edges, then a thick coat of Bondo wet sanded at least a half-dozen times. The results—we'd say just about perfect. Steven Dietz

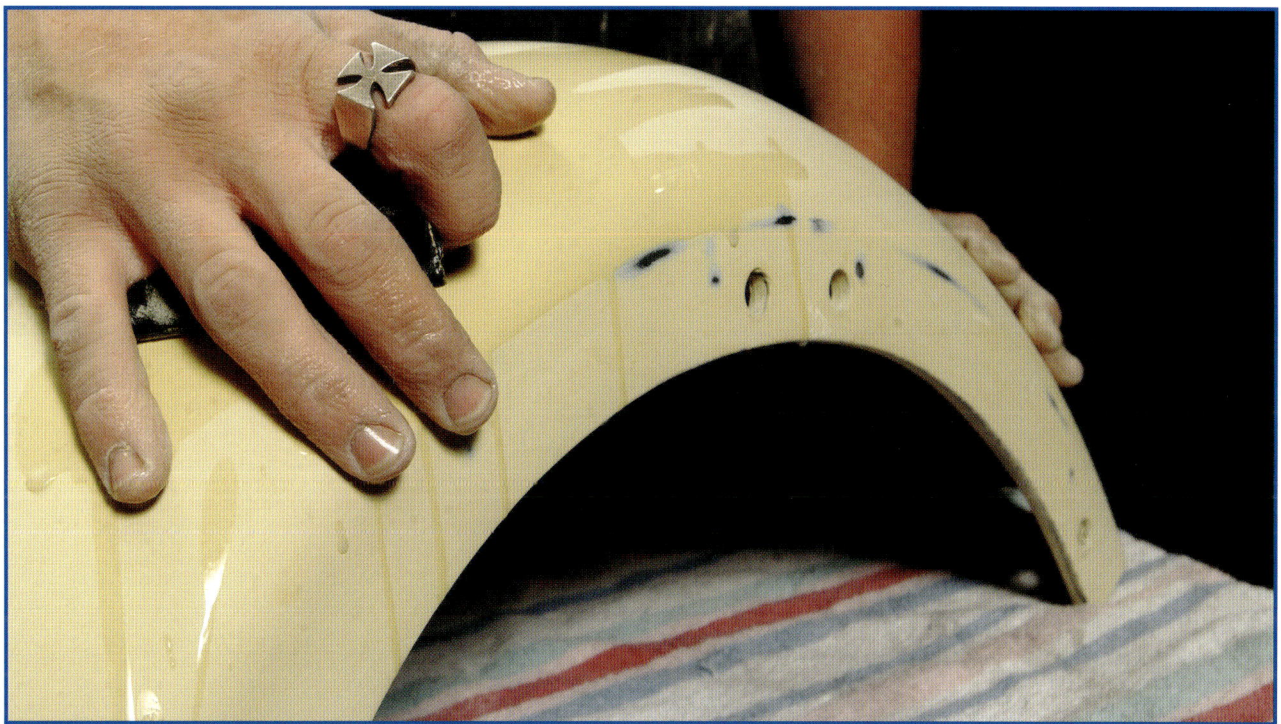

Using the same slow, repetitive technique used to apply and smooth Bondo on the gas tank, we tackled our rear fender. Remember not to leave any burrs or rough edges along fender seams. Steven Dietz

Wet sanding must be done in a warm, clean environment—it helps to have some good music playing or maybe a cold one because you can't hurry this job! Steven Dietz

Now it's the front fender's turn under the putty knife and sponge—note wrinkled hands from constant immersion in water. Steven Dietz

will also require a few hours of fill-in work if you want a chopper that will turn heads and bring home show trophies. Steve rates the West Coast Choppers parts as among some of the cleanest, better-finished steel bits he's seen, as they required far less time under the putty knife than some others he's worked with. The chassis was no exception and he was able to complete the necessary bodywork in just over five hours. This mostly entailed carrying out a slow, exacting inspection of the entire chassis, from neck stem to rear axle and noting where any welds or grinding marks needed smoothing over.

Steve chose to apply body filler to most of the junctions between the various engine and accessories mounts and the frame itself, and around the signature spiderweb frame gusset up front. He was also careful to pop out the retaining rivets in the brass West Coast Choppers logo plate mounted to the neck stem so as not to damage it with body filler chemicals. Molding work will not be necessary on the lower engine and transmission mounts as these will be mostly blocked from view by the drivetrain components. However, the massive box-shaped top motor mount was exten-

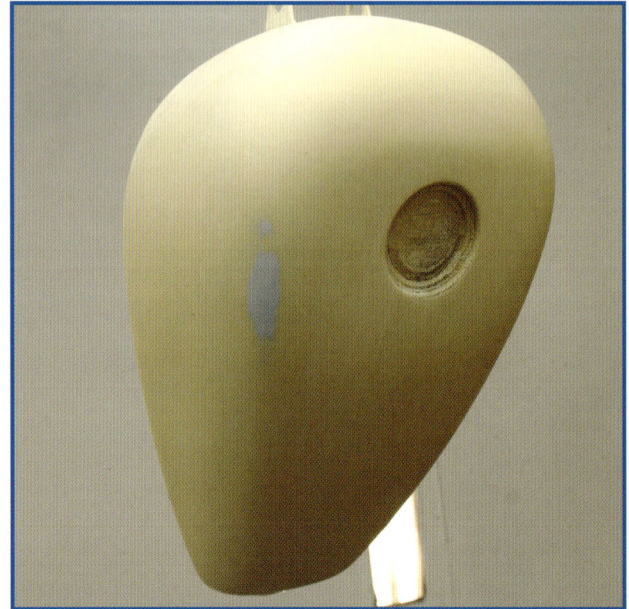

Above and opposite: With the surfaces sufficiently smoothed, the parts are hung in the spray booth to dry—temperatures should be at least 70 degrees for complete drying with little humidity. Steven Dietz

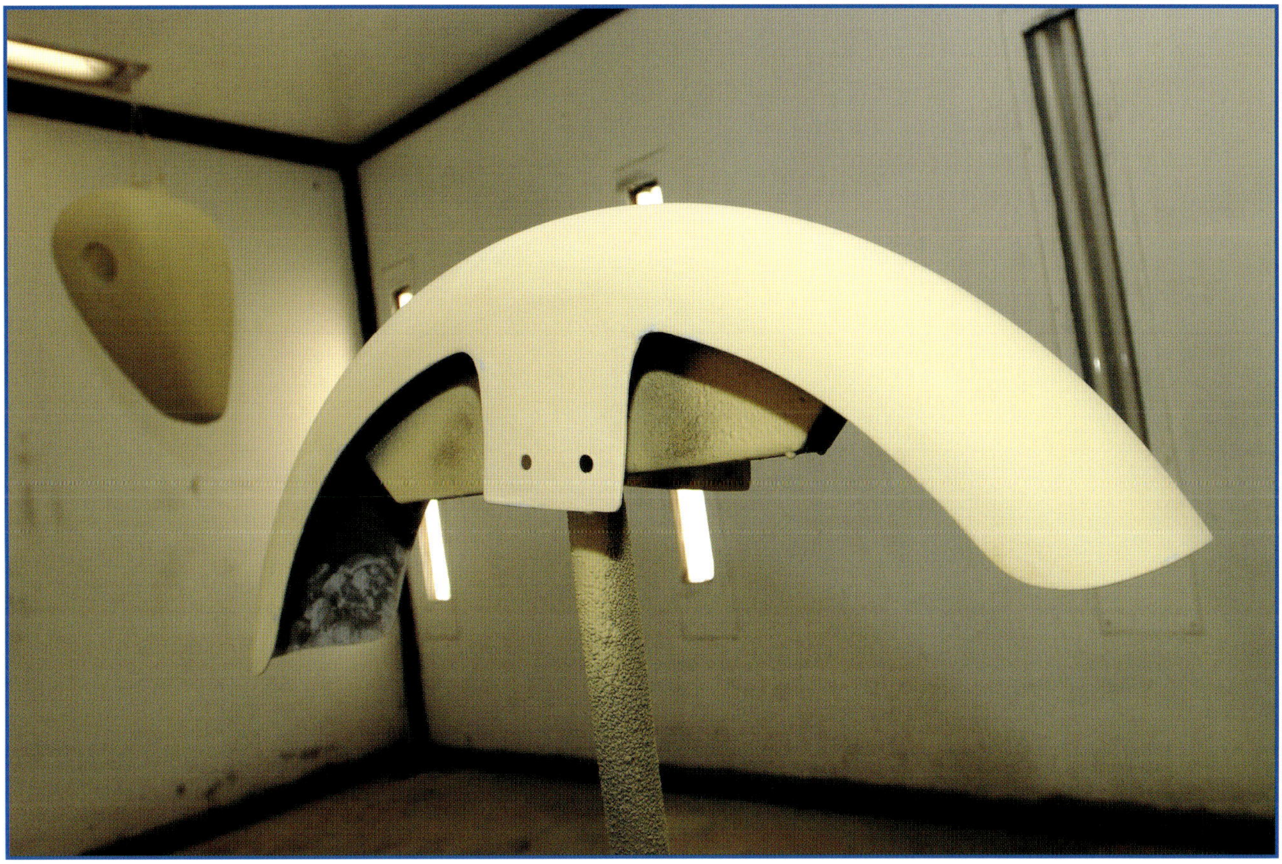

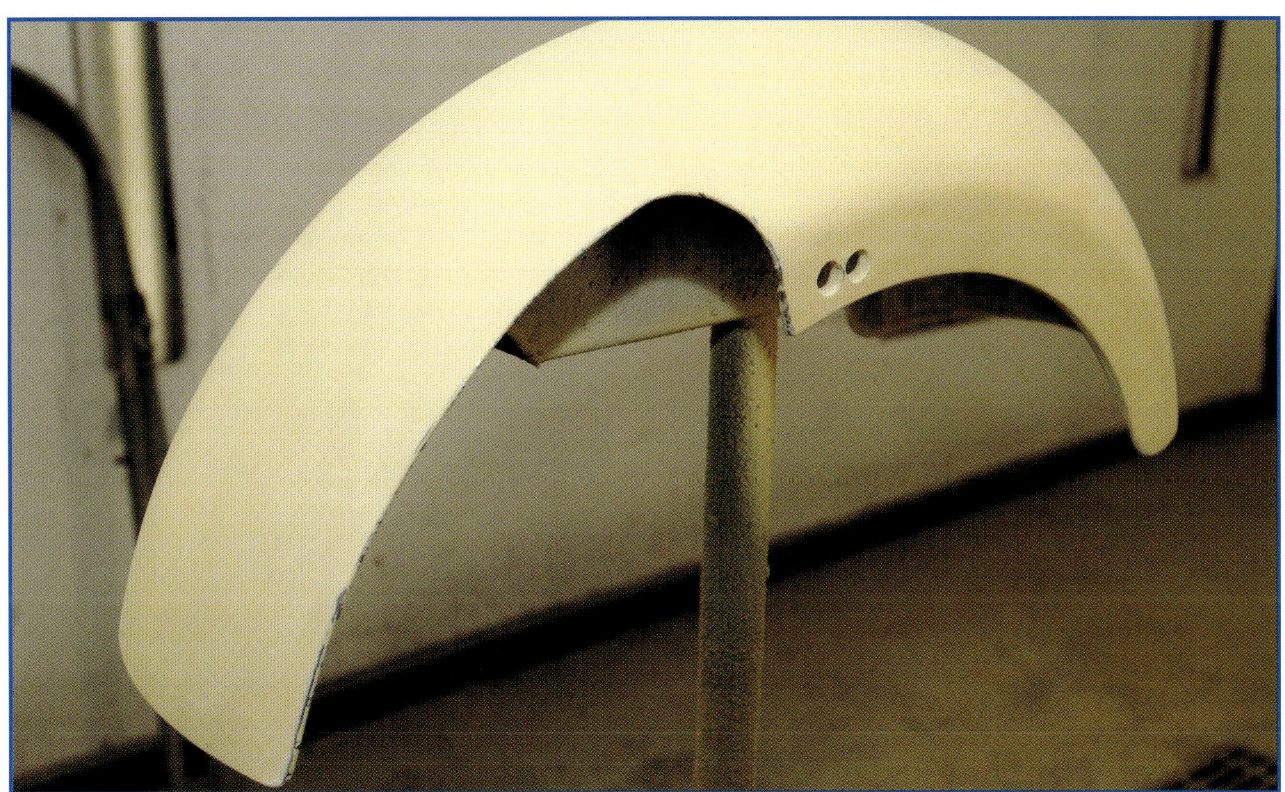

DO'S AND DON'TS

DO: Allow yourself extra time for this step as it can be complicated.

DO: Practice applying body putty to an old fender or piece of sheet metal to practice your smoothing techniques.

DO: Buy sandpaper of varying grit counts as you'll need them.

DO: Wear eye protection when using grinders and sandpaper.

DON'T: Be afraid to correct your mistakes—body filler can easily be re-applied and re-sanded.

DON'T: Cut corners—a cool metalflake paint job won't look so cool on a chopper with grinder marks showing through the paint.

DON'T: Be afraid to call in professional assistance for this step. Good body men are often grateful and eager to get their hands on something besides dented mini-van fenders.

---

sively molded as it will be clearly visible beneath the flush-mounted Sportster-style gas tank. This required covering up the seams along the sides of the motor mount while being careful to leave the central tapped hole clear of overflow material.

Though this work is generally done with a smaller putty knife, Steve, an expert, chose to use his fingers as it was easier to apply the material around the circular frame tubing and into the nooks and crannies near the frame-mounting junctions.

Like the body filler applied to the sheetmetal parts, this, too, will require sanding, this time using a dry technique and 180-grit paper.

Once seams are sufficiently smoothed, take this opportunity to search out any other surface imperfections you might have missed. Steve took the handy handheld electric grinder and filed down a few of the small rough edges remaining on the chassis and made sure the rear fender mounting holes on the hardtail were properly tapped to accept the mounting bolts—this is definitely something you'll want to do before any paint is sprayed onto the bike as you don't want to have to send off any expensive and time-consuming airbrush work to fix something later.

After the frame putty has dried sufficiently and you've completed your sanding, run your fingers over each of the areas you've just worked on for a test of how smooth they feel. Any burrs that catch your skin will have to be sanded away before painting when the transition between bare metal and

Bondo should be relatively unnoticeable.

Though the preceding steps may have seemed unnecessary and complicated, they're not. The entire preparation process is often referred to as "molding" by chopper builders and it's a time-honored custom trick that's been use for countless applications. In the 1960s, many builders like Denver's Choppers and Arlen Ness used fiberglass body filler extensively for covering seams between fenders and frames, and even attaching gas and oil tanks and even the occasional king and queen seat to a chassis. In the most extreme examples, chopper builders used body putty to mold radios and instrument panels into the gas tanks of their choppers or completely cover all the nuts and bolts on their motorcycles with filler so that if anything broke or rattled loose under all that fiberglass the entire bike had to be stripped down to repair it. It can be used to create a wild and almost surreal flowing look that either thrills or repulses chopper enthusiasts. For this chopper-in-a-box project, we've performed some fairly simple molding that should be easy enough for the average builder to accomplish without giving anyone a migraine. But keep in mind, if the step is beyond your abilities, most custom bike shops or car, boat, and motorcycle painters will perform the service for you for a few hundred dollars at most. Regardless of how you achieve smooth finishes on your sheet metal parts and frame, it's a necessary process that more than prepares us for the next step— the spray booth.

DARREN MCKEAG'S RED FLYER C.F.L.

This big, bad, red West Coast Chopper was constructed entirely from scratch by Darren McKeag, an amateur chopper builder. Curious about what sort of full-blown custom bike he could build on an average budget (Darren ended up spending about $20,000) this bike proves that you don't need a professional athlete's salary or a five-record deal to ride a fine piece of iron.

The basis for this bike, like ours, was a C.F.L. rigid chassis picked up from Custom Chrome, Inc. From there, Darren pieced together all the major components he'd need to finish his bike before starting construction, which eventually took just over six months. The rear fender is a 9-inch-wide, Two-Eight model from West Coast Choppers covering a 200-series rear wire wheel with a chromed aluminum rim. The matching front wheel is a good cost-saving move, as is the use of a chromed Harley-Davidson Wide Glide front end. The Hell Bent exhaust pipes have blued and discolored pretty badly in the 2,000 miles of road use this bike has endured, which might have been deterred had the builder coated the inside of each exhaust pipe with a blast of heat-resistant black header paint. The 3.5-gallon Villain gas tank was treated to a red gloss finish with gold flames, which was also applied to the Jesse James Steeler front fender and frame. The tiny solo seat is an aftermarket item, an option worth considering if you want to save bucks over having a custom seat pan fabricated to your liking.

See? You can build a chopper on a budget. Darren McKeag's Red Flyer was built for around $20,000 and features many money-saving elements, such as a Harley Wide-Glide front end, matching chromed aluminum wheels, and an off-the-shelf forward foot controls.

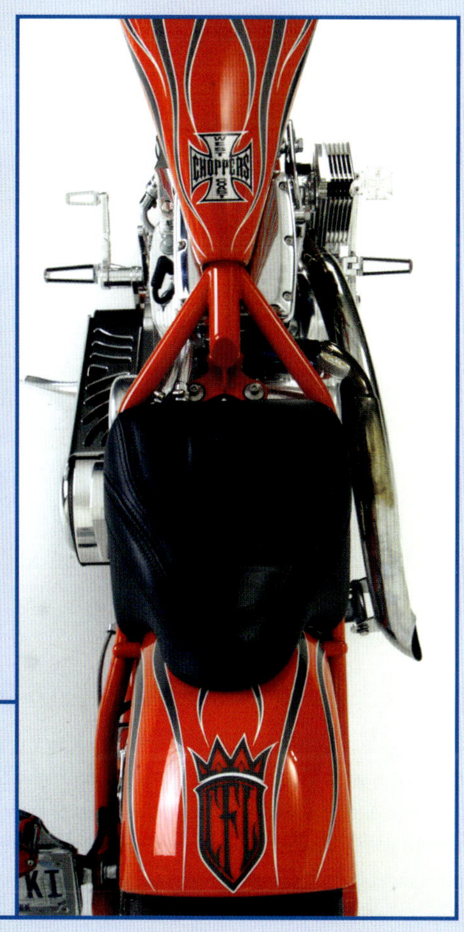

A custom solo seat can cost a good chunk of change. For something that your butt will cover most of the time, it might be worth going the aftermarket route. Notice the discoloration of the pipes. This can be avoided, or at least slowed down, by some heat-resistant black header paint on the inside, but some riders wear their blued pipes as a badge of honor.

With the molding of the frame welds already covered in the last installment, Steve's crew rolled the chassis and sheet metal over to the Steel City paint booth for a session under the spray gun. I'd bugged him for months to paint the chopper an ugly shade of metalflake green with bright orange flames to imitate the paint job on the first C.F.L. chopper I'd ever seen. Steve, for his part, was having none of that.

"Look, Jesse James might have designed the parts for this bike, but I'm the one putting the whole thing together for you. Let me make this thing something that says 'Steel City' just as much as it says 'West Coast,'" he argued. Convincingly, I might add.

Left to his own devilish devices, Steve wasted no time lining up a shade of bright red with so much metalflake the paint salesman asked whether he was planning to paint a bass boat or a chopper.

This was an important discussion to have during any kit bike build because the paint scheme you

PAINTED PARTS

The only rules that apply when designing a paint scheme for your chopper is that there are no rules. This rigid C.F.L. built by Jesse James in 2003 is covered in a neato faux-rust finish, replete with green corrosion marks along the matching fork legs and tiny bronze sculptures affixed to the frame downtubes. It also requires no polishing, you might notice.

Bright red, single-color paint adorns this early West Coast Choppers C.F.L., accentuating the bike's classic chopper lines nicely—a few logos or stickers in place and we're talking an eye-catching custom chopper painted for a couple hundred bucks, tops.

Before hooking up the air compressor in the paint booth, Steve covers the engine mounting holes and other delicate areas of our chassis with protective tape. Steven Dietz

choose for your chopper will be the one component that's A) hardest to change (as it will require disassembling the entire motorcycle down to the bare frame) and B) because it's the most notable visual aspect of any chopper. Steve was correct in persuading me against having my kit bike painted in an exact replica of the Green Meanie C.F.L. feature in Chapter I—choppers are supposed to be about individuality, which has little to do with simply imitating a paint scheme that someone else had already rendered on another bike. Better yet, Steve encouraged me to spend a few weeks pouring over various custom chopper magazines and Internet sites to find inspiration for a unique color theme.

From the various home- and factory-built C.F.L. choppers featured throughout this book, you'll notice that most of the bikes have been painted with either a solid one-color theme or rendered in classic hot rod style with a base color decorated with multicolored flames. Most of these builders are at least uncon-

sciously aware that the customs built at West Coast Choppers tend to follow similarly subtle and understated design themes and they build their bikes to follow suit. Over the years, the elaborate and, let's face it, butt-ugly and tacky mural paint schemes popular a couple of decades ago have mostly faded from view. While there are still a few design-deficient souls found on Main Street, Sturgis, riding fatbikes covered in hokey renderings of flying unicorns, Viking maidens, and other cornball art lifted straight from the cover of a heavy metal album circa 1979, today's choppers benefit from a more sensible approach to custom paint. That said, it's your money and your party, so if you choose to bedeck your Jesse James kit bike in bare-breasted airbrush renderings of Sheena the Warrior Princess, have at it. Just remember that the simpler paint jobs tend to hold up to time and fashion better than, say, a cartoon of Bart Simpson or a silly Confederate flag motif.

Plenty of inspiration for your chopper's finish can

With the bearing already installed in the frame neck, it's necessary to mask off this area as well—paint has a way of invading even the smallest openings, so be careful. *Steven Dietz*

A cleverly designed suspension system helps Steve spray his parts from all angles simultaneously without having to touch the chassis or sheet metal parts during the operation. Home builders can improvise a similar spray suspender by running rope or small-diameter wire through hooks or beams attached to a garage ceiling. *Steven Dietz*

be had from a variety of sources. We looked extensively at custom car magazines like *Hot Rod* and *Lowrider*, the always excellent journal of Latino urban custom culture. Here you'll find endless examples of custom paint tricks that can be adapted to your motorcycle using little more than a photocopier and some imagination. Lowrider trucks are often painted with scalloped designs along their hoods and flanks, and this timeless design was often adapted to early bobber-style choppers back in the day and still works today. Flames and tribal patterns may seem overdone and too common in the chopper scene these days, but by varying the colors you choose—how about, say, orange flames with yellow ghost flames underneath on

a blue, instead of black, background, for instance—it's still possible to create a new twist on an old favorite.

After piecing together our kit chopper in a rolling chassis form which was sprayed with a coat of black primer, many folks complimented us on creating such a "classic, cool, and unpretentious chopper." Flat black finishes, as seen on some of the sportbikes built by Italian firms like Aprilia and Ducati for instance, are weather-resistant, require little in the way of cleaning and maintenance, and can be touched up easily. For the brief time our bike remained in the primer-coated rolling chassis stage, we pasted a couple of massive chrome-mylar West Coast Choppers stickers across the gas tank and we had to admit the stark con-

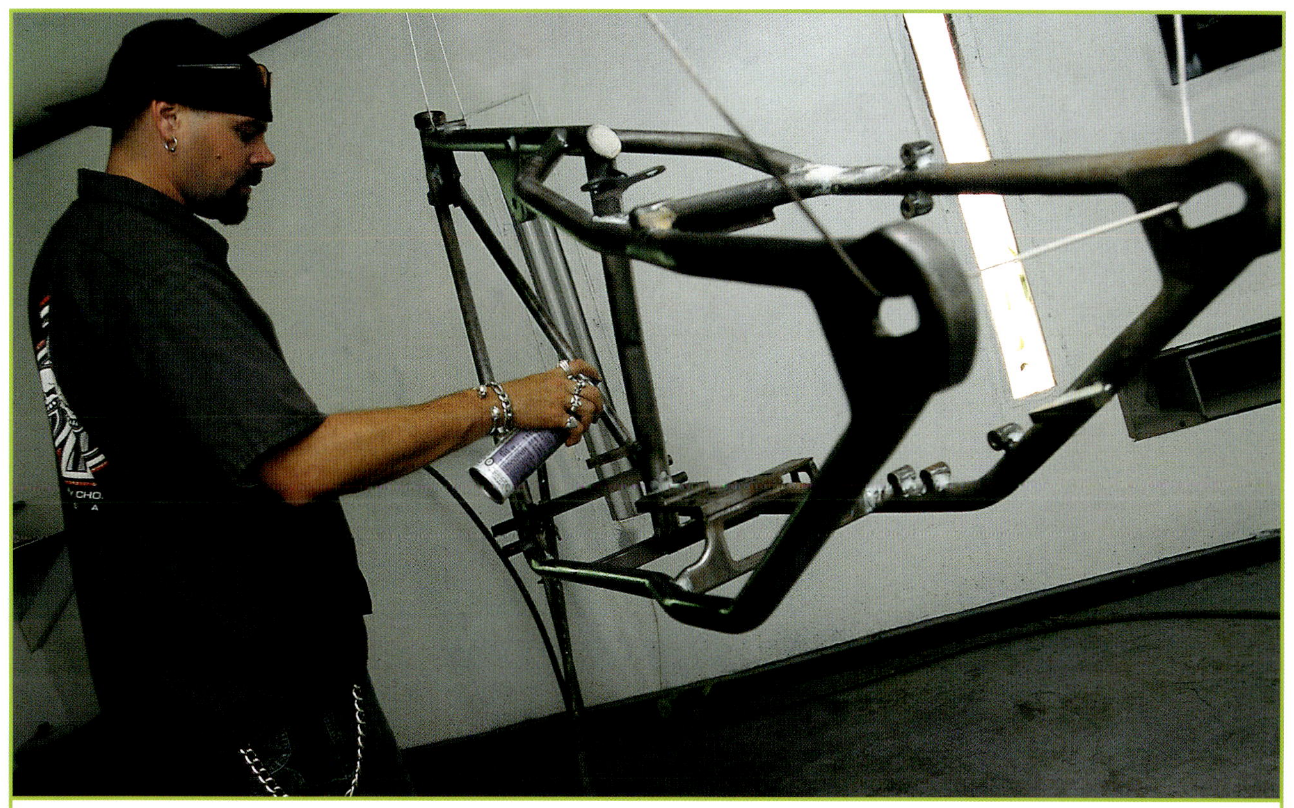

A grease-cutting aerosol solvent is applied to make sure there's no oil left on the frame from last chapter's body molding sessions. Wipe areas clean with a fresh towel afterward. Steven Dietz

trasts of the highly polished engine and chrome detailing, along with the black powdercoated Perse front end did look damn cool.

Jesse James himself has used flat black finishes on some of his own C.F.L. bikes, most famously the rigid chopper ridden in the Discovery Channel's *Motorcycle Mania II* documentary, opting to black out the fork legs and engine for a wicked, sinister look. Another groundbreaking West Coast look to be considered by home builders is the chromed bodywork/painted frame option. The *El Diablo II* Jesse James built for the 2001 Camel Roadhouse promotional show at Daytona Beach Bike Week capitalized on this theme with a frame that segued from metallic blue to a jungle green, with bodywork triple-dipped in show chrome. This was a clever and effective reversal of the finish on the original chromed frame/painted bodywork *El Diablo II* featured in the aforementioned Discovery Channel documentary.

Chroming a motorcycle chassis can be an expensive process—we called several prominent national chroming firms and found prices for dipping a rigid frame in the shiny stuff to run around $2,000, Softails run about $2,500 including swingarm. This option will really make even the simplest single-color basecoat on your sheetmetal parts look striking, though you'll need to pay careful attention to the various mounting points on the chassis, most of which will require a complete re-tapping after a dip in the chrome bath.

There is a popular movement sweeping the chopper scene where motorcycles are built with elaborate themes in mind. Some incorporate fantastically detailed hand-fabricated parts to replicate props from popular films—sword-shaped sissy bars inspired by *Lord of the Rings* come to mind—while other builders spend months designing mural paint schemes chronicling historical events like wars and Wild West themes. While these designs are all a matter of personal taste, we've always liked West Cost Choppers for their decidedly spare and unadorned appearance. There isn't much in the way of ostentatious ornamentation on a Jesse James chopper, just an engine, a place to sit and some well-shaped hard parts. From a design

Some small amounts of surface rust have gathered on the chassis from sitting inside a humid workshop during the warm summer months. Go over all rusty areas with some fine emery cloth until bare metal is showing through as paint and rust don't get along.
Steven Dietz

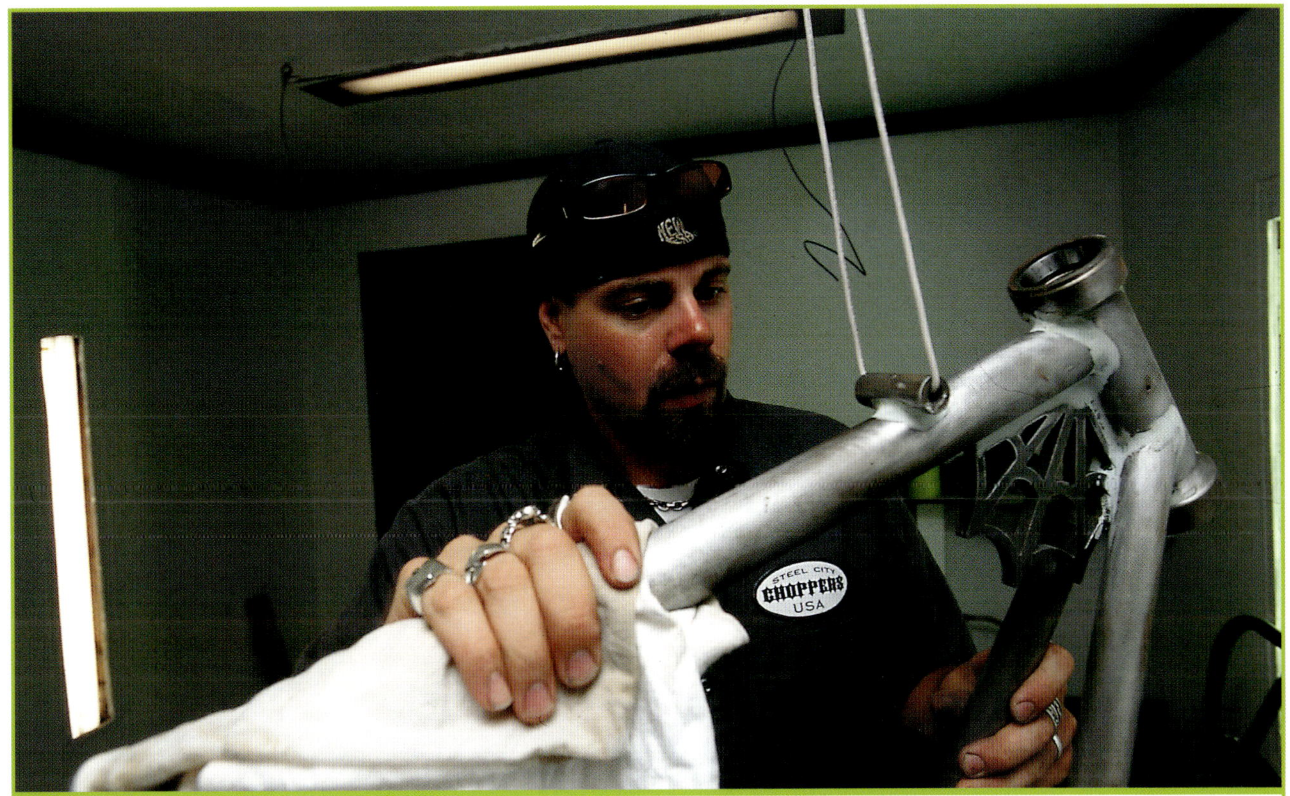

The last thing to touch the surface of your chopper's chassis before the primer coat should be a cleaning cloth—fingerprints will come back to haunt you later. Steven Dietz

standpoint, they bear more in common with, say, a rail dragster from the 1950s or a 1932 T-bucket roadster than a million-dollar concept car from a Detroit automaker. Keep this ingrained simplicity of design in mind when designing your home-built chopper.

Choosing a paint color and type is, like selecting chopper parts themselves, a tough job made even more difficult by the sheer number of options currently on the market. Many of the wilder, more eye-catching paints like lacquers, candy finishes (notable for their "wet" look) and pearls will not hold up to direct sunlight as well as some of the more recent chemical-based paint compounds. This is worth considering if your motorcycle will be built and ridden in a Sun Belt state. Acrylic-based urethane paints will serve a warm-climate chopper builder better as they tend to withstand the effects of sunlight, harsh weather, spilled gasoline, and polishing chemicals. Lots of builders have considered spraying their choppers in those wacky neon or day-glow paints popular on racing bikes, but be forewarned that they seldom hold up to the sun's rays as well as, say, a candy or pearl finish.

Eventually we settled on a paint scheme we found to be both familiar and original. I was dead set on a metalflake base coat which Steve agreed on. Only, instead of green, we settled on a bright red basecoat with the same orange and yellow flames I'd requested originally. Steve also decided the chopper would really stand out from the crowd if he painted additional matching flames along the frame's front downtubes and on the top motor mount as well. I'd inquired about some bling'd-out lettering on the frame rails as well, imitating a style I'd seen on ghetto-fabulous custom cars and lowriders over the years. Detailed hand-lettering on a motorcycle can be very cost-prohibitive I soon learned and, turning my attentions to the Internet again, I found several graphics shops aimed specifically at motorcyclists (www.the-image-works.co.uk is an excellent source for all kinds of logos, lettering, and designs on die-cut weather-resistant vinyl) that would render everything from a West Coast Choppers logo, color-matched to my bike's paint, to some goofy lettering that we'd place along the lower frame rails.

Above and opposite: The rolling chassis in flat black primer and stick-on decals. Some observers commented that we might have left our C.F.L. in this partially finished state for a cool, early hot-rod look, similar to the dusky black C.F.L. with the Wasp-style gas tank featured in the adjacent photo. We didn't.

Lucky for us, Steve is a talented painter, having attained an art degree somewhere in between long bouts chopping motorcycles, so he let me watch as he laid down a masterful display of hand-laid flames. The flame designs that would later be rendered in a vivid orange and yellow are first drawn onto the primer covered gas tank and fenders—and, in this case, even the top motor mount and frame downtubes—and then followed over with painstakingly laid outlines in very thin masking tape. Curling the tape along the contours of the sheet metal is not something the at-home chopper builder is advised to do—unless they're extremely patient at correcting foul-ups.

Let's walk through the basic setup and procedure points for custom painting your West Coast Chopper, following Steve "Do-it-all" Peffer through a day in the prep and paint booth.

First of all, each and every part to be sprayed with primer and paint must be clean of any contaminants like oil or dust. A quick wipe-down with a solution of water and a good, grease-cutting cleaner (even mild dishwashing liquid will suffice) and then a thorough drying with a terry cloth towel should do the trick.

Steve has a specially constructed spray booth at his shop, so there was no worry about the paint getting contaminated by dust or flying debris (even bugs) as there would be in a home garage. This means if you absolutely must paint your bike at home, try to make sure you can seal off the garage doors with plastic sheeting to catch any foreign particles circulating around your spray area.

Ideally, the place you work should be good and balmy—any temperature below 70 degrees Fahrenheit might compromise the adhesive and drying qualities of your paint. Cold air is usually wet air and any moisture on your parts, even very small amounts of moisture undetectable to the naked eye, can wreak havoc on your paint and primer once its sprayed.

Warmth is just as essential as dryness. OK, you're thinking, "I'll just unplug the space heater from the attic and bring it to the garage while I paint my chopper, right?" Well, not exactly. The problem is, space heaters and closed rooms full of paint fumes can be a lethal combination, so we suggest only spraying on a warm spring or summer day. The space should also be well ventilated because the overspray lingering in the air around a freshly painted motorcycle can do more damage to your lungs than three packs of Luckies a day! This also means a respirator mask (available at your neighborhood pharmacy for a few bucks) and eye

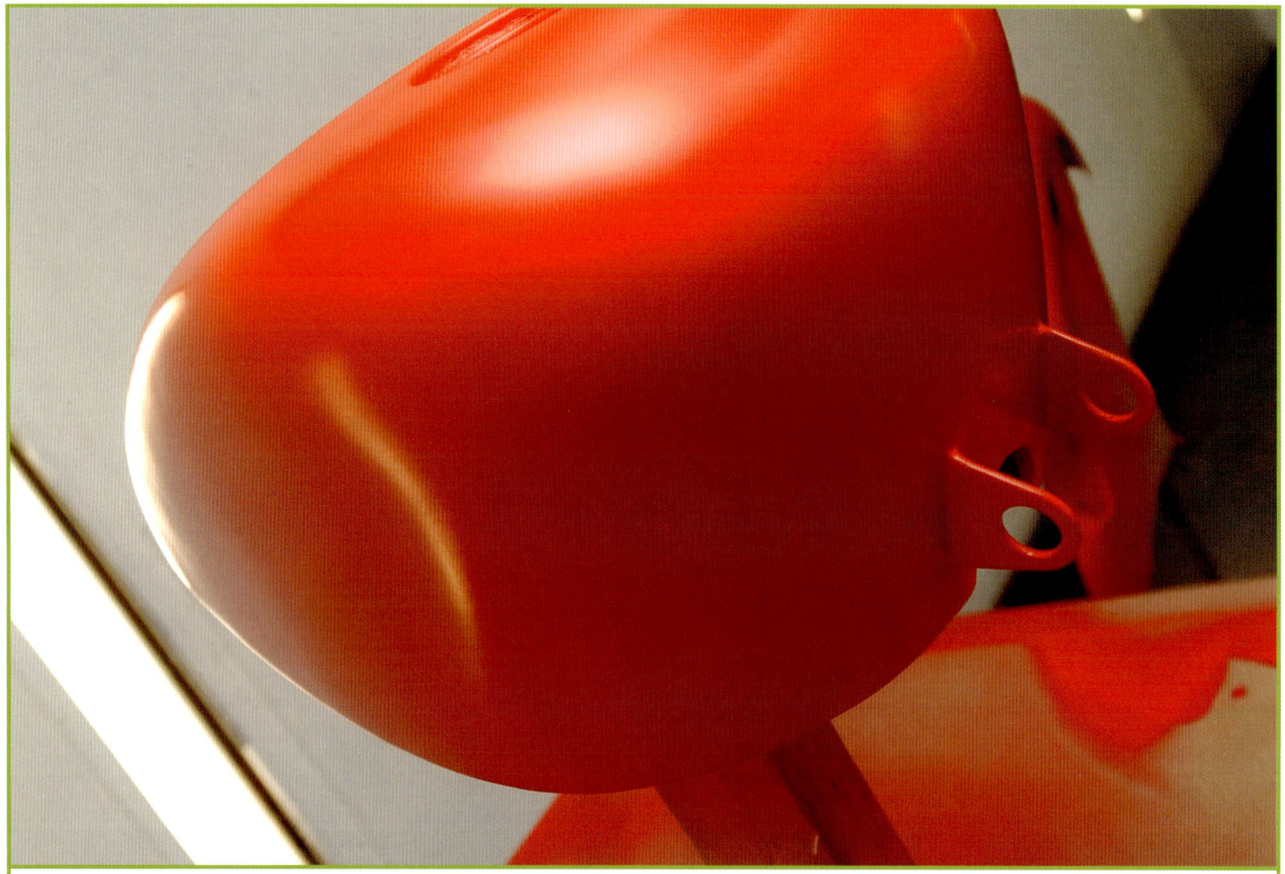

Holding the spray gun six to ten inches from the surface of your parts and using a slow, easy back-and-forth motion should result in a smooth, even coat. Steven Dietz

protection are essential for every step of the painting procedure.

Using a spool of medium-weight steel wire, suspend the frame from the ceiling in the center of your garage or spray booth. This method bypasses any need to lift or turn the wet frame during spraying, which would leave ugly fingerprints and smears in the finish. The wire suspension system also allows the painter to rotate fully around the motorcycle, saving time and providing access to the underside and all surfaces simultaneously. Steve chose to spray on a urethane filler primer which cost us about $150 for a half gallon, but is among the better primers available. Working rapidly with the gravity-fed spray gun held about six to ten inches from the frame and sheetmetal parts, Steve laid down a good three complete primer coats, affecting a solid layer of black over the bare metal frame and the putty-covered sheet metal parts. Flowing, even, back-and-forth motions are what works best here, and when finished, the parts should have that dense, flat-black appearance of a piece of charcoal.

The primered parts are then pulled down from their wire perches and wet sanded with 400-grit paper to smooth out the highly porous finish of the primer coat. You don't want it too terribly smooth as some porousness is necessary to make the paint stick, but concentrate on smoothing over any small holes or imperfections. Each part is cleaned with a new, dry cloth dampened with Acrily-Clean, an effective wax and grease remover.

The next day, Steve re-hung the sheet metal bits and was ready to apply a DVC basecoat of bright PPG red. Four coats were sprayed on followed by another wet sanding with 400-grit paper before we began applying the heavy metalflake. This solution is actually a clear coat infused with the tiny metal reflective bits and comes premixed from famous West Coast Choppers collaborators House of Kolor. The metalflake mixture is then blended in with a PPG urethane clear coat (DVC 500 series) which is used to

Note the even red tone along the spiderweb frame gusset and downtubes. After primary coats are applied, the sheet metal and chassis are left to dry overnight after a thorough wet sanding with fine-grit paper. Steven Dietz

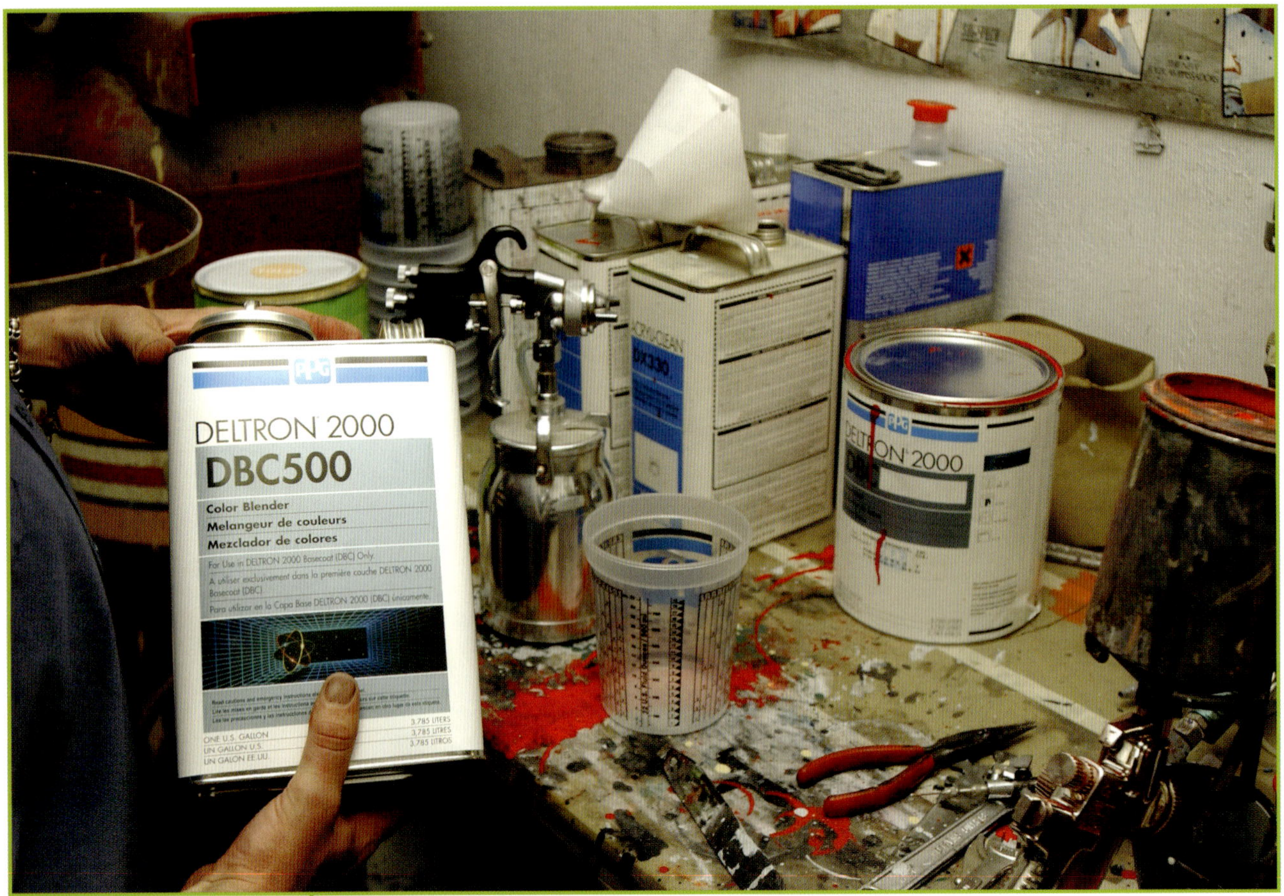

The next day, leftover dust from last night's sanding and any particles floating around in the drying booth are cleaned off with solvent. Always use a new, clean cloth. Steven Dietz

Steve begins mixing the red metalflake finish coat—have your paint supplier select the proper amount of metalflake, which can be tricky to work with for first-timers. Steven Dietz

The thick, coarse metalflakes can easily clog even the most powerful spray guns, so... Steven Dietz

Steve uses an old hot rod car custom painter's trick—he adds several glass marbles to the mix cup. These will be shaken frequently during the painting process to help keep the flakes churning with the paint. Steven Dietz

Each part will require a good dozen or so passes with the metalflake before Steve creates the desired depth of finish. Steven Dietz

Flaked, sanded, and waiting for tomorrow's session with the flame tape. Steven Dietz

Thin, single-sided tape like this 3-M Fine Line Tape is perfect for laying out flames, scallops, or other designs on sheet metal. Again, a few practice runs if you're new to custom painting may be in order. Steven Dietz

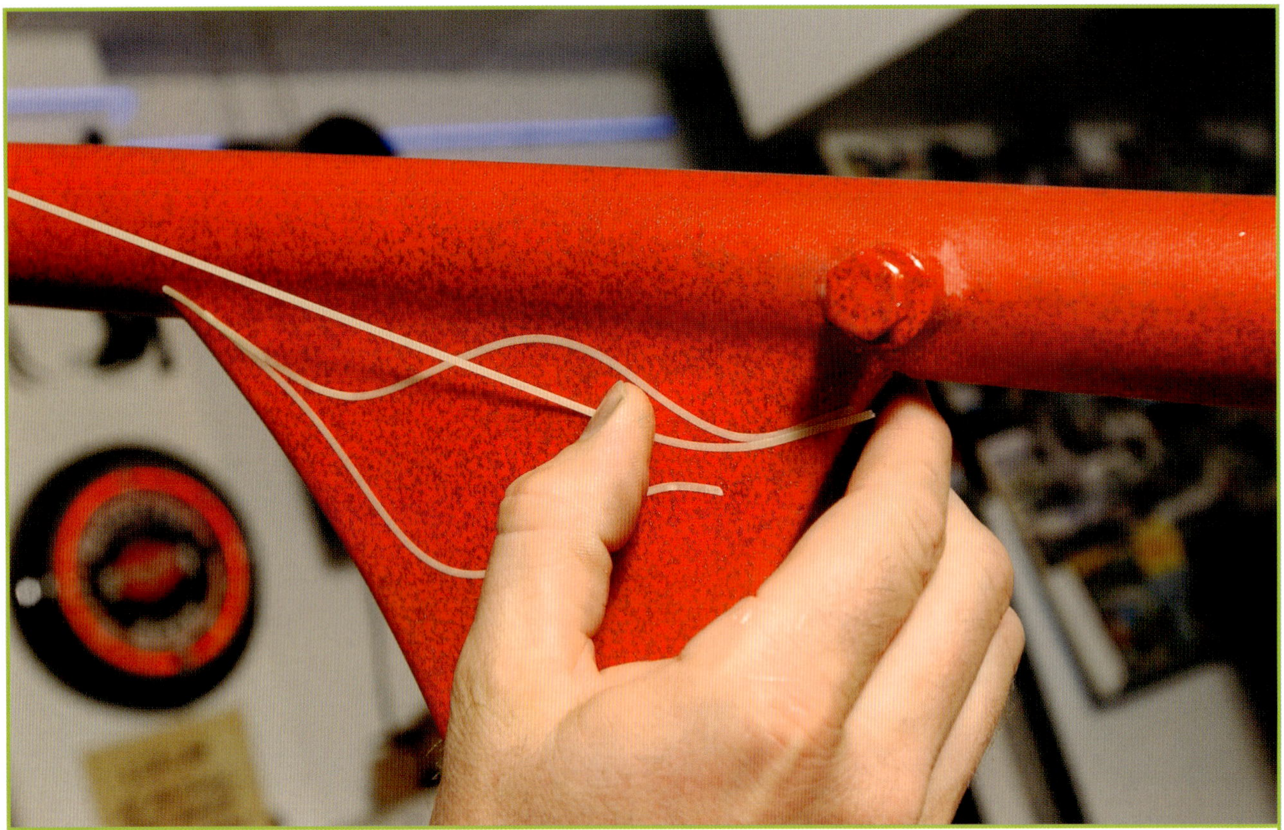

A delicate touch was required to apply extra-thick flame tape to the motor mounts on our C.F.L.'s top motor mount. An experienced painter, Steve laid the tape by hand, unlike most painters who cover a surface in tape and then draw on the flames with a marker before cutting out sections to be painted with an X-Acto knife. Steven Dietz

Here, Steve displays his taping technique on the hood of a custom pickup truck shot with the same color of red metalflake as our project chopper. Pliable tape can be removed and bent to a painter's desire several times. Steven Dietz

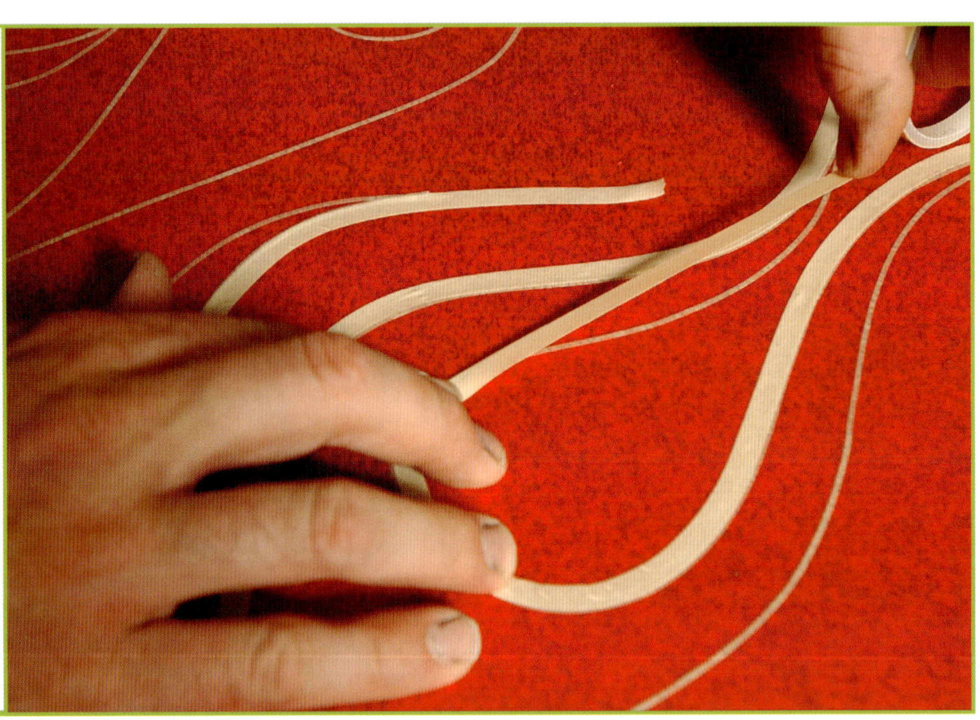

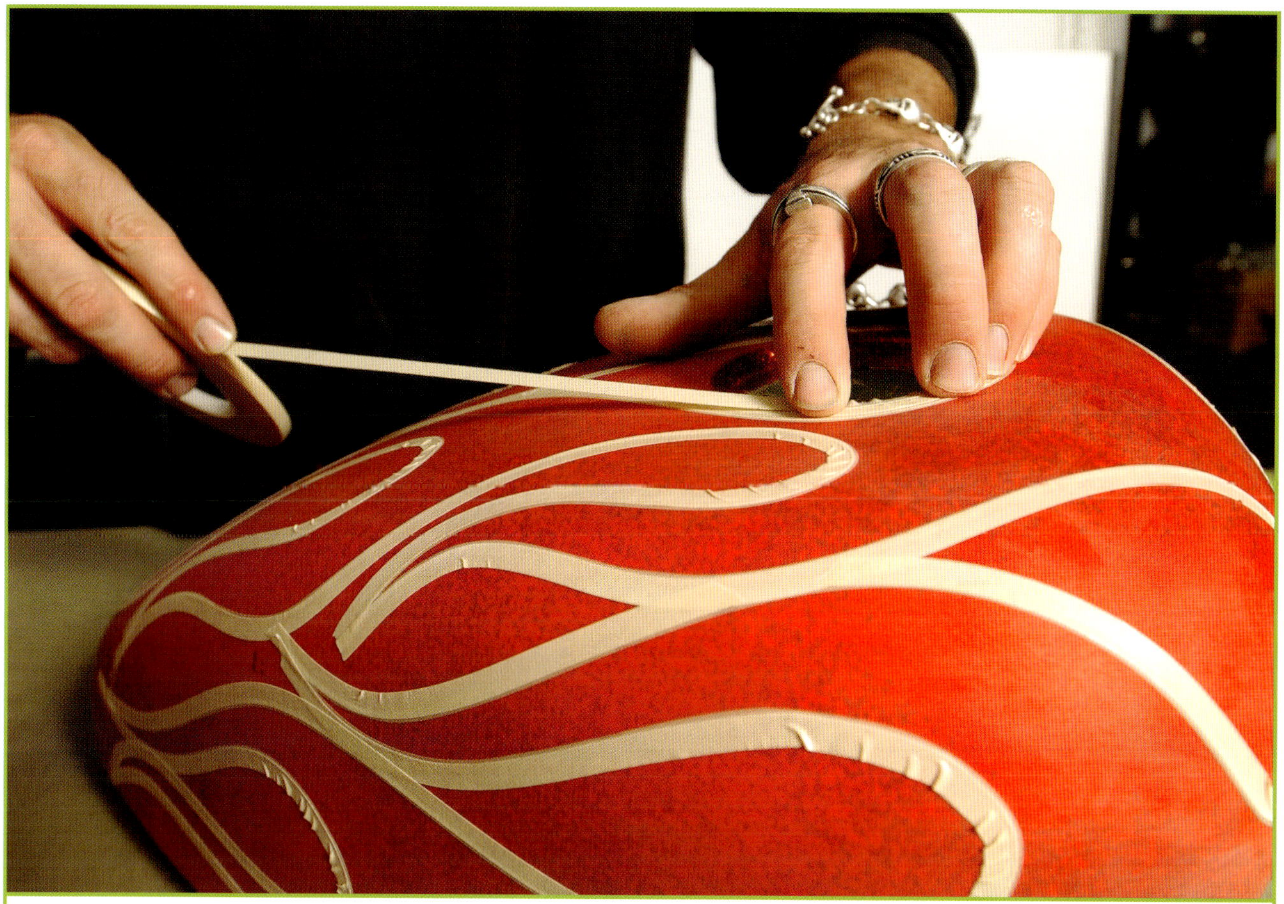

The chopper's Sportster gas tank and fenders all taped and ready for the spray booth. Again, remember to clean off any hand grease or residue from the taping session with solvent before spraying. Steven Dietz

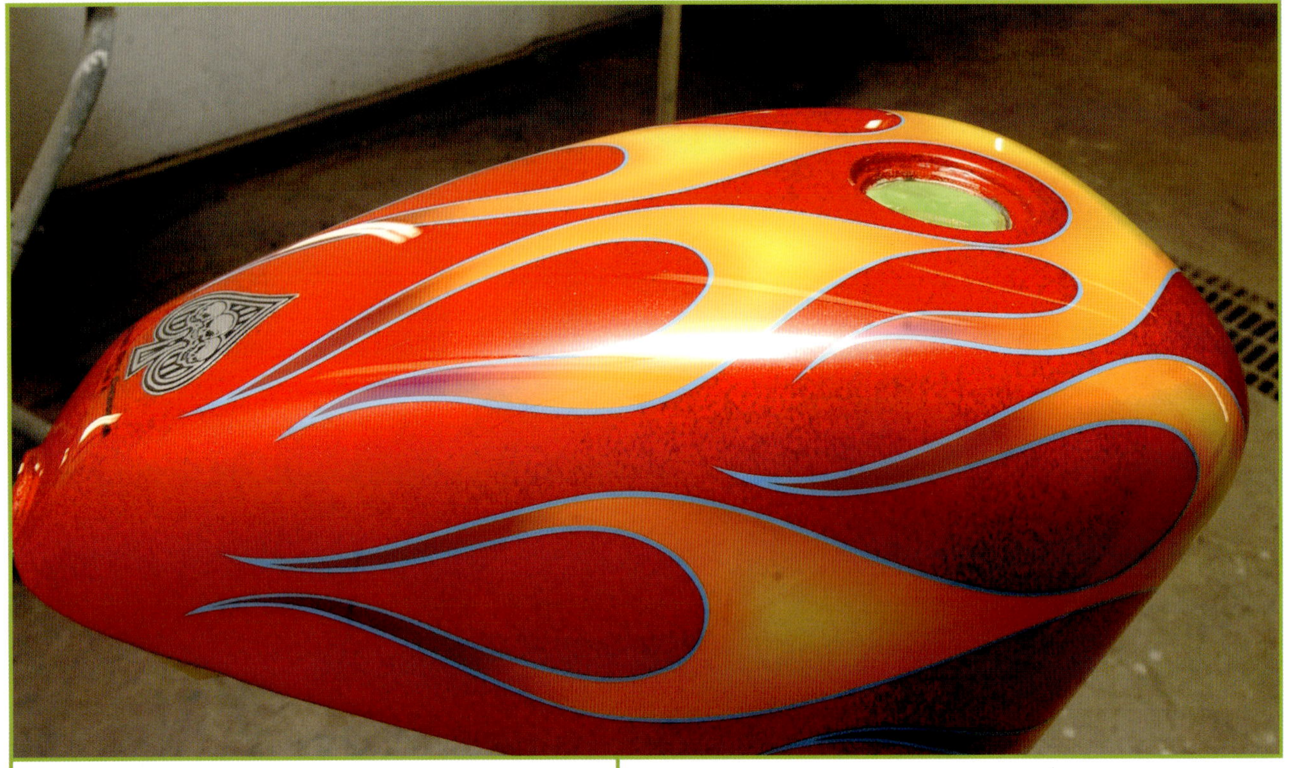

House of Kolor yellow flames with light blue edging courtesy of Steel City Choppers; 13 coats of clear were added, each one individually wet-sanded before this perfect finish was achieved. Steven Dietz

help the flakes adhere to the surfaces of the chopper parts. This is not a process for the faint of heart or impatient as Steve spent the better part of a full week spraying as many as 15 coats of the metalflake over the red basecoat until the proper level of flashiness was achieved. Steve filled the air-powered spray gun's gravity-fed reservoir with small glass marbles, an old custom-car painter's trick, dating back to the days of Von Dutch and Ed "Big Daddy" Roth. This helps keep the thick paint and its metal cargo from becoming congealed by shaking the spray gun gently and frequently as he went. Each coat had to be left to dry for a couple of hours (see directions on paint jars for length of drying period and relevant air temperatures) before the next was added. Once the desired finish was achieved, Steve then used his hands to gently pad down the tiny flakes of metal along the frame and bodywork, making sure none of the hard particles was left standing on end to damage the clear coat.

Next comes the clear-coat urethane, which Steve applied in three even layers. These were also wet-sanded, this time with extremely fine 500-grit paper until a shiny surface began to take form. It's important to remember to apply your successive coats of paint promptly after sanding as the freshly sanded surface will accept paint more easily. If you're wondering, as I did, why so many coats of paint were added, Steve says the depth or richness of the paint on any chopper is directly linked to how much time the parts spent in the spray booth. We've all seen motorcycles painted with hardware store spray cans and the flat-looking 1967-Nova-on-blocks finishes are always bad. So take as much time as is necessary and remember the cardinal rule of custom painting. You can never have too many coats or too much time invested in this, one of the most important parts of your chopper.

Though it may not seem as if you'll ever get there, eventually you will achieve a finish on your metalflake and clear-coated surfaces that's satisfactory. At this point, Steve began masking and cutting the taped outlines that would create the flames running along the bodywork and frame downtubes. Flame masking is a deeply involved process taking several attempts to get anywhere even close to correct, so it goes without saying that you should either practice this quite a bit before attempting it on your own or hire a professional. Base coats and clear coats may require little more than the ability to keep your spraying arm moving in a steady and controlled manner to cover surfaces evenly, but flames are one of the toughest parts of custom painting.

Steve Peffer perfected his hand-laid flame masking technique on an old Honda CB 450 chopper that he built back in high school so, by this point, the process is pretty much a matter of eying up the desired surfaces and carefully bending the narrow lining tape to fit. The trick that most custom painters use is to cover an entire gas tank or fender in masking tape, cutting away the flame patterns after they've drawn them into the tape with a marker or wax pencil. Steve's steady hand managed to painstakingly lay each line out and then used a roll of very thin 3M masking tape to cover the adjacent sections of the frame and bodywork that were not being flamed.

Three individual coats of yellow base are laid down (with wet-sanding in between) followed by a coat of House of Kolor Tangelo Orange with yellow airbrushed tips on the flames added for dramatic effect. A meticulous craftsman, Steve finished the job with an intense session of thin pinstriping to create the bitchin' light blue borders surrounding the flames on every surface.

When we say this motorcycle looks as good—if not better—than anything we've seen from Anaheim Avenue, we're not just spewing hype, as it has drawn inquiries at every place we've ridden it concerning the professional quality of the paint finishes. Of course those working on tighter budgets can achieve their own levels of painting mastery using rented spray guns and less involved detailing. But if it's show trophies and attention you're looking for, professional paint is the way to go. Of course before we wow the competition, we've got some long nights in the garage piecing together all the chromed and painted parts that make this chopper a complete motorcycle. Which is where we're heading in Chapter 5.

DO'S AND DON'TS

DO: Wear a respirator mask and eye protection whenever working in the spray booth—the mist from a spray gun can damage your lungs in no time.

DO: Clean all surfaces with Acryli-Clean wax and grease remover between each sanding session. Even the tiniest particles of dust and grease can ruin a paint job.

DO: Your own thing. There are no rules when it comes to designing the paint for your West Coast Chopper, so do some research.

DON'T: Paint your chopper in a cold or non-ventilated garage. The temperature should be at least 70 degrees Fahrenheit. Cold air brings moisture that can ruin paint.

DON'T: Skimp on supplies. You don't want to run out of your favorite color halfway through the job.

DON'T: Neglect to stock up on fine-grit sandpaper. You'll need to wet-sand your surfaces in between each successive coat of paint.

CHRIS GATEWOOD'S BLACK 2003 C.F.L.

Builder Chris Gatewood special-ordered his West Coast Choppers C.F.L. rigid frame with an additional 2 inches of stretch in the front downtubes, creating a radical upswept look reminiscent of the balls-out Swedish choppers popular in the 1980s. Gatewood utilized some interesting and inventive custom trickery in building his dream bike, which boasts a high-performance, 80-cubic-inch mill and a springer front end. Few springers appear on the bikes built at West Coast Choppers, but this one, a 10-inch overstock black anodized model from Denver's Choppers of Henderson, Nevada, looks perfectly suited to this stretched and flamed chopper. The 60-spoke wheel rims were treated to an orange powdercoating finish to offset the black paint with orange flames, which the owner even managed to match with a set of orange Axcell plug wires for his dual-plugged S.T.D. heads and Harley-Davidson cylinders. There's even an orange Maltese cross and tribal design stitched in the custom-made solo saddle.

It seemed a prudent move to hop up his stock 80-inch motor rather than stress the rigid frame with an engine of 100-cubes or more; the bottom

end starts with a set of heavy-duty Delkron cases, with the S.T.D. heads polished and ported for improved combustion and flow. A Mikuni 42-mm carb is hidden behind the W.C.C. Maltese cross air cleaner while the Hell Bent pipes on this machine seem to have held up to regular use quite well.

A serious road version of the classic C.F.L. rigid (as evidenced by the tool pouch strung across the front end), Gatewood's chopper is equipped with some top-flight parts to ensure a reliable ride including a Jim's close-ration 5-speed transmission, Performance Machine four-piston brakes, and a BDL 3-inch open primary drive with a neato slotted belt guard. Home-built bikes like this are living, fire-breathing proof that cool custom choppers don't have to break the bank to be roadworthy.

CHAPTER 5
FINAL ASSEMBLY OF YOUR CHOPPER

DRIVING TOWARDS HOME

With our frame and bodywork all painted and the final clear coat wet-sanded and polished to a high gloss, we are ready to begin final assembly on our West Coast Chopper. Just as with bolting together the major components for a rolling chassis, the final build process involves simply (*OK, maybe not simply*) retracing the earlier steps. Only, this time, the motorcycle's electrical system, fuel and oil lines, and drivetrain components have to be fully operational.

We first placed our two wooden balance blocks atop the lift stand, this time covering them both with a clean terry cloth towel to protect the freshly painted frame from being nicked. Placing the painted frame on the blocks, we set about remounting the forks fol-lowing the same procedure used in Chapter 2, with the following of some important extra steps: This time, when installing the top and bottom neck bearings, they'll need to be packed with a good waterproof grease (like the type used on boat trailer axles) or, if that's not readily available, a standard bearing grease as found at most auto parts stores. When re-assembling the forks, allow the lower legs to dangle over the edge of the lift stand to keep the chassis level during installation. And be sure to use a thread adhesive like Loc-Tite on all of the major suspension parts and engine bolts during re-assembly, and don't cut corners when it comes to tightening each bolt to recommended torque specifications. Up top, take this time to secure the handlebar risers into the fork while the bottom

Following the same path as when we constructed the rolling chassis in Chapter II, we begin final reassembly of the painted sheet metal parts, powertrain, suspension, and chassis. First comes the rear fender, which this time bolts on easily. Steven Dietz

Front fork assembly with triple trees and front wheel is attached as a whole. Steven Dietz

The support blocks we installed on our worktable come in handy yet again—cover all support mechanisms with cloths to protect paint at this stage of the build. Steven Dietz

Steve carefully scrapes away excess paint that's gathered inside an engine mounting hole - good thing he caught it just in time! Make sure your accessways are clear before hoisting the engine into the chassis. Steven Dietz

With protective tape aligned throughout the freshly painted chassis, the engine is hoisted into place from the right side of the motorcycle. Extra hands are quickly employed to support the massive block as the mounting bolts are secured. Steven Dietz

Next, the Twin Power transmission is bolted onto its mounts while the clutch plate of the Primo belt drive is installed from the opposite side. Lock-Tite thread fastener is a must-have for this level of installation, as is a good-quality torque wrench. Steven Dietz

clamp is out of the way. Next, install the fork's mainshaft by sliding it into the neck from below. Steve recommends tightening the side pinch bolts in the lower triple clamp securely and the bottom nut to about 40 foot-pounds—but not much more, as you'll want to allow free movement and avoid compression on the bearings, which may hasten wear.

We'd purchased a pair of fender spacers from West Coast Choppers, which turned out to be a good call—the front fender has a narrow profile and, without the spacers, would have come up about a half-inch short of meeting both sides of the fork's lower legs. With the spacers in place atop the mounting holes, the fender mounts up easily. After this, the front wheel is installed with the rotor attached to the left fork leg immediately thereafter. Make sure the brake rotor spins freely with the caliper installed and check to ensure there's no sloppy free play in the wheel—if so, you may need to have a shop cut you a few spacers to

shore up the wheel on your axle. And make sure there's still precious daylight showing between your tire and the fenders. Tires swell at road temperatures, and the last thing you'll want to find is two parts rubbing against each other in the passing lane.

After torquing the riser bolts beneath the top clamp into place, install the handlebars, which you can use to help move the machine around during the final build stages. We affixed our GMA clear anodized master cylinder and matching clutch and brake levers ($414, complete) and a set of nifty chromed handgrips (swap meet, $50) to see how the completed front end looks: Bitchin', to say the least.

Once the front wheel, bars, and accessories have been properly installed, the entire chassis and fork assembly should be shifted rearwards so the front wheel can be secured in one of the stand's wheel chocks for support. With our new set of mounting holes drilled in the rear fender, we bolted it to the hid-

Steve test-threads the bolts that will hold the oil tanks and battery box in place on the chassis. These aluminum parts can occasionally crack from vibration stress so nylon lock washers are a great idea for securing them in place.
Steven Dietz

Oil tank goes in next; remember to cut a small piece of foam rubber to use as a base cushion for the battery so it doesn't split from excess engine vibration. Steven Dietz

den mounts with the four setscrews provided in the C.F.L. kit. Using one strong friend (or a couple of not-terribly-strong ones), lift the rear end of the motorcycle and slide the rear wheel (with tire), brake rotor, and caliper-mounting bracket through the axle slot. The axle may require a little encouragement to pass through the frame, which can be done with a soft rubber mallet.

Steve had purchased an offset sprocket from a Harley-Davidson FXRS, a clever trick that helps wider rear tires fit into close quarters like the rear of our C.F.L. frame. The FXRS sprocket is beveled in design, which places the sprocket's teeth about ¼ inch farther away from the rear tire and allows a flawless installation of the 200-mm rear Metzeler tire. The new fender mounting adjustments proved true and the rear

105

Starting to look like a finished motorcycle—remember to photograph your progress as many state D.O.T.s require complete documentation of home-built motorcycles. Steven Dietz

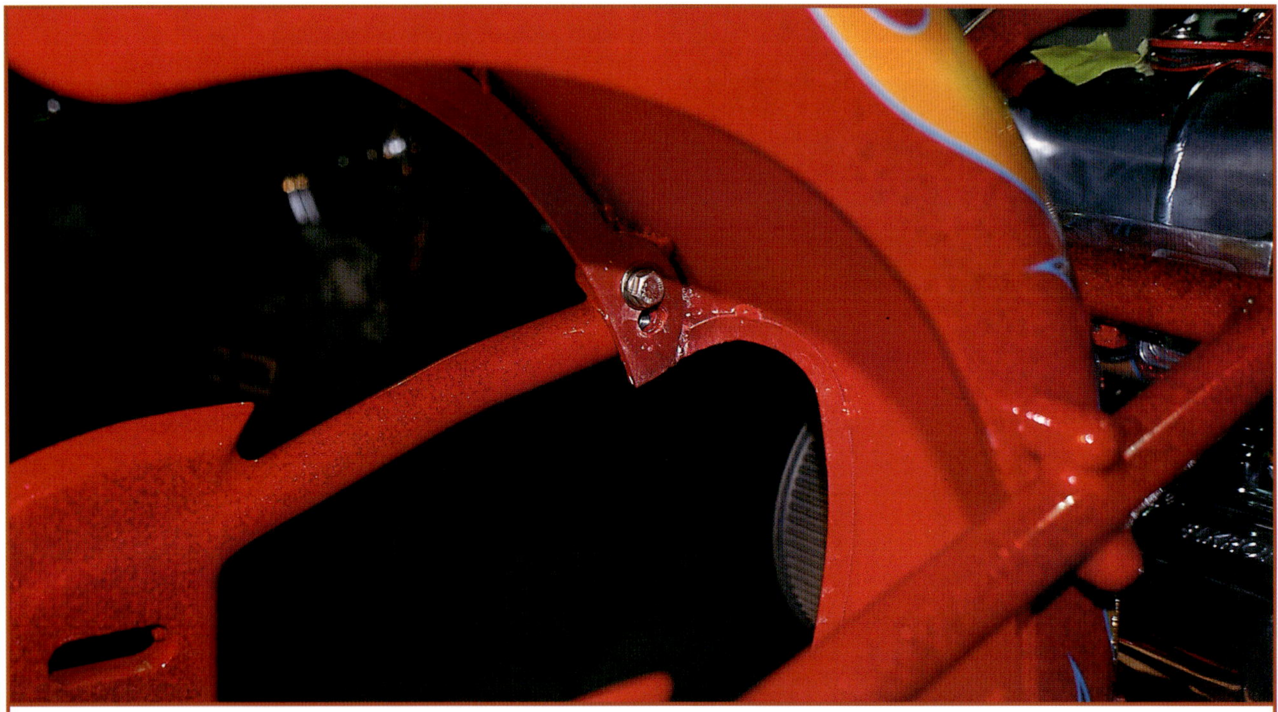

This close-up shows our modifications to the rear fender to correct a manufacturing error with the mounting points—double lock-washers will help keep these expensive parts safely secured to your chopper. Steven Dietz

Steve remounts the gas tank onto the frame after re-tapping the top mounting hole. Novice and intermediate builders may want to skip the wearing of wristbands and watches that might gouge paint. Steven Dietz

While some builders cut corners by skipping the paint on the bottom on the gas tank and insides of fenders, the judges at your local bike show sure won't. The extra time it took to finish this tank will go a long way toward bringing home trophies. Steven Dietz

wheel spun freely; we'd wait to bolt on the Maltese cross axle covers until the final drive chain had been properly adjusted with the installation of the Primo belt drive and the front drive sprocket.

Moving forward along the chassis, Steve bolted down the Sportster gas tank, affixing the chromed Pingel fuel petcock to the threaded mounting hole on the left side. Make sure to blow out the gas tank with compressed air to remove any residue from the masking process during painting, and the use of a silicon-based tank sealant (available at most bike shops for about $10) is always a good idea—you don't want to find a leaky weld seam after the motorcycle's been covered with an expensive paint job. We saved a few pennies by using rubber fuel line which can be had for about $4 per foot at most bike shops. Cut to length, it cost about $2.50 from the petcock to the S&S carburetor. At this point, Steve paused to line the inner frame rails with a strip of yellow masking tape, which protects the freshly painted chassis during the engine

and driveline installation process.

Lifting the engine about chest high, Steve walked it into the frame from the right side, placing the engine atop its motor mounts, which shop assistant Jared Steithner quickly bolted into place. The Midwest powerplant includes torque specifications for each of the engine mounting points, and we can't stress enough the importance of getting your nuts in order, so to speak, especially with an engine of this size (or larger) which vibrates a great deal at speed. Again, you'll want to apply a thread-securing paste like LocTite to each fastener, including the bolts securing the top chrome motor mount we picked up from CCI for $173.

Next, Steve slides in the Twin Power five-speed transmission, which was first topped off with fluid via a narrow plastic funnel inserted into the chromed cap screw atop the tranny case. Moving around to the left side of our quickly emerging chopper, Steve starts on the re-install of the belt drive kit; first the clutch plate

Moving back up front, Steve begins attaching the front GMA brake caliper to the left Perse fork leg; the braided-steel CCI brake line is attached at the caliper with the bleed valve opened for filling the line and master cylinder with fluid. Steven Dietz

is attached over the transmission shaft using the four long hex-head bolts, followed by the front motor plate which is mated to the engine using a similar mounting system. Both pulleys are mounted over their respective shafts while we also attach the starter extender—a shaft made to turn over the engine via the transmission—which is attached from the left side, above the rear pulley. Tighten, but don't overtighten, all of the belt drive's bolts at this point, as both pulleys will need final adjustment after the clutch has been installed and adjusted for free play. Install the rear drive sprocket for the chain first and then the clutch basket, or rear pulley, first (Primo includes detailed instructions in each kit for clearances, etc.) before sliding the belt over the rear pulley and clutch assembly. After slipping the front pulley into the belt, secure it onto the main engine shaft with the pulley nut, using a straightedge or level to ensure the pulleys are in perfect alignment with each other. You'll need to fiddle with your belt drive/rear chain for alignment and tension adjustments, and make sure to have everything "just so" before torquing down the clutch hub and engine shaft nut to specifications.

Real hardcore chopper pilots will skip the mounting of the Primo chromed aluminum belt guard (included in each kit) though we recommend using it for several reasons: We've known riders who've collected road grime, debris, and even small stones into their open belt drives, which can chunk teeth from a pulley faster than you can say "$500 deductible," and catching a pant leg in a drivetrain isn't exactly something you'll want to explain to an emergency room doctor! Better yet, the belt shrouds can be etched, painted, or detailed in any way your imagination desires, adding an affordable and easy custom touch to your West Coast Chopper (more on this in Chapter 6).

Next up come the clutch and brake cables, the former routing with help from a set of simple parts store zip-ties from the right side transmission case to through the engine bay and on to the GMA level

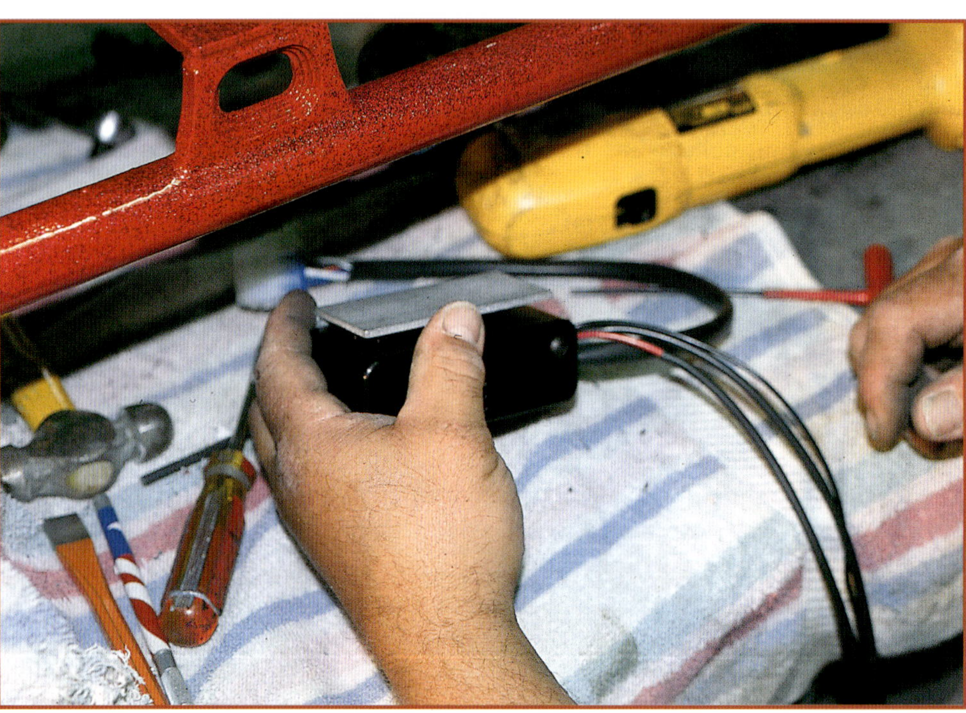

Note the lock washers installed in between the front fender mounting bolts and the fender— safe means no accidents.

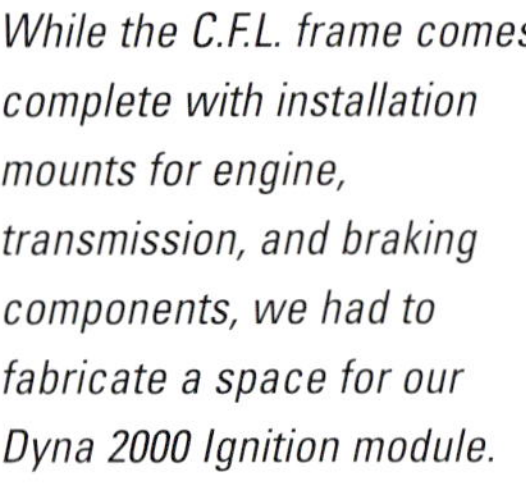

While the C.F.L. frame comes complete with installation mounts for engine, transmission, and braking components, we had to fabricate a space for our Dyna 2000 Ignition module.

Here, Ace wrench Big Bob Miller improvises by drilling a hole beneath the main transmission mount. He'll later thread this hole (upside down, no less!) and tap it for the ignition mounting point.

assembly located atop the left handlebar. A CCI throttle cable hooked into the feed on the S&S carburetor and into our GMA throttle housing—the free play should be adjusted only slightly, the remainder to be worked in after the bike is fired up for the first time and the idle adjusted accordingly.

Finally, we fitted our Ness Tech chromed side-mount kickstand ($199) to the front motor mount, pulling the retention spring over the nub with a flat screwdriver. The Ness Radius forward foot controls came back on, remembering to fill the rear master cylinder that's part of the brake-side control with Dot 4 fluid before re-attaching the unit to the motor mount. When mounting brake calipers and attaching hydraulic lines on any custom motorcycle, the brake fluid (which is highly corrosive so watch your custom paint and chrome around this stuff!) must be "bled," or drained, from the master cylinder through the

Even the best-planned choppers can run into problems: this Big Boar battery had enough juice to turn over the Midwest El Bruto 113-inch stroker motor, but it proved too tall to fit beneath our custom seat. Some builders have solved this issue by running sealed-cell batteries that can be mounted horizontally in a battery compartment with no fear of corrosive acid leaks.

hoses and into the calipers in order for the brakes to work properly. This is one of motorcycle building's most tedious jobs and, like foreplay, few men actually care to invest the time. But without carefully allowing the fluid to flow through the master cylinder reservoir where any trapped air can be forced out, the brakes will be about as scary as those old drum hub brakes on early choppers in the 1960s.

Steve Peffer invested about two hours between bleeding both of our chopper's brakes. Start by loosening the small bleed valve located on the front caliper. Then, remove the two screws on the top of the front master cylinder mounted on the right handlebar and slowly pour a small amount of fluid in. As the fluid flows through the brake line, periodically pump the brake lever until tiny air bubbles surface in the master cylinder's fluid. Using a catch basin beneath the front caliper and an assistant, re-tighten the bleed valve once fluid starts to come through. If there's still air in your brake lines, you'll know it when you squeeze the brake lever and it goes all the way back to the handlebar without any resistance. Likewise, you'll know when all air has been forced from your lines because a pull on the lever (or a stamp on the rear brake pedal) meets with a firm, progressive resistance. It's actually easier than it sounds and just requires a little patience to get right.

SPARKS WILL FLY

Setting up your chopper's electrical system has been made far easier for today's at-home chopper builders, thanks to the availability of pre-packaged electrical wiring kits that include color-coded wiring harnesses covering everything from plastic connectors to

Making sense of several yards of black spaghetti; the Dyna 2000 ignition fits conveniently inside the El Bruto's points cover; we had to purchase a complete charging system (voltage regulator, stator, alternator) which was installed on the motor while the chassis was being painted.

enough wire to hookup your handlebar switchgear to the starter button, coil, ignition, and lights. Though several aftermarket companies offer complete wiring harnesses for chopper builders, including Pro One and Drag Specialties, we chose a kit from CCI ($132) that was designed for a late-model Softail. The harness includes wires one foot longer than stock for reaching the control switches on taller handlebars and other custom applications, though our chopper would be running only minimal electrical gear, no switches—just a headlight, taillight, and starter—in the best tradition of West Coast Choppers.

After eliminating the wires that would have been used to power turn signals, the handlebar-mounted kill switch, and horn, Steve routed the thick, remaining cluster of wires through the conveniently located channel running the length of the frame backbone.

The C.F.L.'s wiring tunnel includes a hole in the bottom, just above the top boxed motor mount for running wires to the starter and coil, and another just before the frame neck for supplying power to the headlight. The unnecessary handlebar wiring was simply snipped clean with a set of crimping pliers (remember those from Chapter 1?).

While lots of riders prefer to have a starter and kill switch mounted on the handlebars as a convenient means of cutting power in an emergency, we opted for a starter button located in a hole we drilled in the left side of the battery box. Easy to reach while seated in the saddle and cleaner in appearance than even the tiniest handlebar switches, it allows us the option of cutting power by simply switching off the ignition key that we've mounted beside the coil between the cylinder heads. This is another delicate area of your chop-

Open view of the business end of the S&S "D" series carburetor: the West Cost Choppers Maltese cross air cleaner fit easily due to a specially made backing plate.

per's construction where it may not be a bad idea to seek professional help. No one can doubt your chopper credentials for allowing a licensed Harley mechanic to have the final say over the intricate routing of connectors, relays, and lighting currents, and it's far better to enlist a skilled mechanic at this stage of construction than when your chopper suffers a potential electrical short circuit on a dark highway at 2 a.m.

For instance, the battery I chose to power the C.F.L. was your standard-sized Yumicron Softail cell from CCI ($69.95), which fit into the small, rectangular battery compartment with ease. Once we were sure the battery fit and we picked up a set of heavy-duty rubber-coated Mega Cables from CCI, we placed the battery on a piece of ¼-inch-thick black rubber sheeting (found at any auto parts store for about $3) and cut a cushion pad to fit beneath the battery. Not only would this keep the fragile plastic battery case from vibrating against the metal battery box, it would keep the fluid from shaking under road use and potentially spilling out and damaging the paint. But when we attempted to turn over the massive-stroke 113-cubic-inch Midwest El Bruto engine during test-firing, the stock-output battery was not up to the job. After much gnashing of teeth, head-scratching and the occasional beer break, we opted for a high-output Big Boar dresser battery ($149) designed specifically to fire hard-starting, high-compression stroker engines. This taller, and slightly wider, battery just barely fits within the confines of the West Coast battery box and also required a re-casting of the custom fiberglass seat pan we'd had built (more on that in Chapter 6). Builders who choose to craft their at-home West Coast Chopper using stock-displacement Harley-Davidson engines will encounter none of these types of problems, though it's a matter of affordabi-

Sometimes you have to improvise: the coil of our Dyna 2000 ignition and key plate didn't exactly match up easily. Here, Bob displays a spacer cut from a piece of billet aluminum that gapped the two pieces together for a perfect fit.

DO'S AND DON'TS:

DO: Be sure to apply thread adhesive to all major nuts and bolts. Torque specifications can be found either in a manufacturer's instruction booklets or on their Internet sites. When all else fails, pick up the phone.

DO: Apply masking tape to frame rails when re-installing engine parts into a freshly painted frame. You can also protect your gas tank and fenders while turning wrenches on nearby components with shop towels or T-shirts.

DO: Ask a professional mechanic to assist you with wiring your chopper for electricity if the job feels too difficult. Better safe than sorry.

DON'T: Overtighten banjo fittings on brake lines—this will cause corrosive brake fluid to leak out during use, possibly damaging your paint.

DON'T: Forget to top off all fluids. Midwest's Ultima motors are pre-run at the factory so there's no fear of seizing a new motor, but not all motors and transmissions are shipped filled with fluids.

DON'T: Panic. This a huge step in bringing your chopper to life which may take weeks, even months to complete. Be patient and seek help if your toolbox or experience doesn't stretch as far as you'd thought.

lity and personal taste as to whether an easier electrical hookup will be enough to offset the stock engine's somewhat wheezy 50 or so horsepower.

Other options we discovered, only in retrospect, involved using a sealed-cell no-maintenance battery. These more expensive power cells can be mounted flat on their sides, as there's no fear of corrosive battery acid escaping, and therefore would permit the seat pan to be mounted with no modifications—unfortunately, chopper building as an art comprises much trial and error and it's best to keep an open mind when searching for solutions to these sorts of fitment problems.

We also ran into a mounting hassle when it came time to mount the Dyna 2000 ignition coil to the top motor mount. The coil proved too bulbous to fit beside the larger surface area of the El Bruto engine's oversized cooling fins, so Steel City's resident fabrication expert Bob Miller had to machine a _-inch block-shaped spacer to allow placement of the coil.

We bolted on the Hell Bent exhaust pipes, careful to use a light chrome polish to wipe clean any fingerprints from the build session. The oil on your fingers can turn blue if not cleaned off an exhaust pipe, Steve warned, so we didn't want to take any chances with a set of pipes costing over $1,000.

Next came the installation of a CCI Universal Oil Lines kit in braided steel which proved a perfect fit for the 113-cubic-inch motor. The lines are supplied with integral, threaded fittings that slipped onto the oil pump and engine nipples easily—make double-sure that the lines are attached in the proper sequence with the return feed flowing in the right direction and no kinks in the lines (rare with braided lines, which is one of their advantages). We then topped off the oil tank with four quarts of 20W40 Harley-Davidson oil; the engine had been pre-started at Midwest before shipping so there was enough oil in the mill to make sure our initial starting procedure would go smoothly. Meanwhile we placed the Big Boar battery on charge to ensure we'd have enough spark to start the bike when the time came.

Besides those few hassles, the rest of the final rebuild came together as smooth as a Luther Vandross CD. The throttle cable, brake lines, and lighting system were all simple bolt-up matters, the only detail being a careful and time-consuming bleeding of each of the GMA brake calipers to ensure there was no air trapped within the lines. The advantage of using as many parts from one manufacturer's line came to the surface again and again as we needed to manufacture no spacers, adapter plates, or re-drilling when it came to the West Coast Choppers components (besides the rear fender.)

We did find that we'd scrimped and saved a little too frugally at one point as the $49 swap meet Maltese cross taillight and license plate assembly we

The hollow tunnel of the C.F.L. chassis provided a routing space for electrical wiring. Hole had to be drilled out early on during our build.

picked up turned out to be of such inferior quality, it would have vibrated apart with the first power pulses from our stroker engine. Steve, instead, convinced me to fork over the extra cash for a wicked and very stylish side-mount taillight and plate holder assembly from Pro One. Bolting directly to the Primo belt drive, it cleans up the chopper's rear end and leaves no exposed wiring whatsoever. We'd worry later about legalities like rearview mirrors, speedometers, and whether we'd pass a state vehicle inspection—for now we were pleased to have come so far in such a short amount of time.

During any chopper build project, fully expect to have to farm a few of the tougher parts of the rebuild process out to more, shall we say, skilled hands. Lucky for the marginally gifted mechanics among us, there are plenty of small and extremely capable chopper shops who can tackle all or part of your budgeted West Coast Chopper construction for you, and at a labor rate typically far cheaper than that charged by your local H-D dealer.

"The rebuild came along so easily because we'd gotten all the testing and fitting-together of parts out of the way when the bike was still in bare sheet metal," Steve explained during the rapid rebuild process.

Besides a couple of small setbacks and late-night parts runs, the sheet metal, wiring, engine, and driveline components came together in just under four

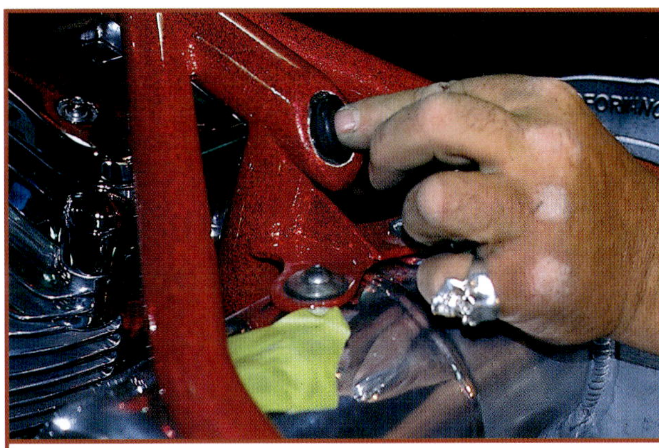

A rubber grommet is installed to cushion the delicate electrical wires from contact with metal parts.

weeks—an impressive schedule to keep, even without any Discovery Channel cameras rolling. Our next step, starting and riding our C.F.L. bike, would prove the most rewarding; but before we did that, Steve let his creative monster out of its cage and had a little fun tricking out our chopper in his own, inimitable manner.

"You can build a bike that looks like it just came out of West Coast Choppers, or you can invest a few days and some sweat and really make it your own," he'd proclaimed.

What he came up with is the stuff that sets show-winners apart from the also-rans.

SCOOTER SHOOTERZ C.F.L.

Some chopper builders are never quite satisfied with even the most radical designs, which is why Lowell, Indiana's Scooter Shooterz' custom shop removed the rear end of this West Coast Choppers frame and replaced it with a wider hardtail capable of holding this whopping 240-millimeter radial tire. The low-riding fender with the tasteful and subtle tribal design rides scarcely a quarter-inch or so above the tire, which is not a custom modification we'd suggest to at-home builders; too many variables can affect the safe operation of a chopper's running gear and woe be to the rider who picks up a serious piece of road debris with no fender clearance to speak of!

That said, this machine is no slouch when it comes to outright performance, as it's powered by a stump-pulling, 124-cubic-inch S&S Super Sidewinder motor, with a slick updraft manifold to support the Force air cleaner. The Santee L.A.F. (Loud As Fuck) pipes have been wrapped in heat-confining fiberglass tape, an old hot rodders trick fabled to seal in exhaust header heat and therefore aiding combustion. Typically, the transmission runs an open belt primary drive with its final drive operating via a thick 520 O-ring chain. In the spirit of the quick-steering C.F.L.s to emerge from the West Coast Choppers garage, this bike runs a relatively short set of roadracing-style inverted forks with powerful drilled Performance Machine disc brakes at both of the 120-spoke wire wheels. Short, stout and bristling with power, this chopper is about as serious as a set of rusty brass knuckles.

CHAPTER 6

THE DEVIL'S IN THE DETAILS

MAKING A KIT BIKE YOUR OWN

While it may be the goal of many at-home chopper builders to create a West Coast Chopper kit bike that is easily mistaken for one from Jesse James' small-volume assembly line, enough can't be said for making that bike on your own. Sure, who wouldn't enjoy the recognition and glamour of everybody thinking your machine was the result of a two-year waiting list and more cash than it takes to rebuild a small Mideast country? But from the very early planning stages of our chopper project, chief builder Steve Peffer has insisted we add a few unique custom touches that shout to the world "Born in Long Beach, Made In Pittsburgh."

Steve always seems to have a few clever customizing tricks up his sleeve and we'd discuss a few ideas while the main construction of our C.F.L. was underway. For several previous show-winning choppers he's built, Steel City Choppers' signature design detail has been an iron Devil's tail that curls menacingly around frame rails, under gas tanks and from the back of his axle covers. Steve envisioned a pair decorating the rear section of the rigid West Coast frame and ended up getting so involved in the bolt-up construction process that he'd painted the chassis before finding inspiration—and some spare steel sheeting—to make his signature mark on this bike.

Steve quickly set about cutting two pieces of 16-gauge steel into what looked like oversized arrow heads. After carefully measuring the contours of the frame's triangular axle junction, Steve used a marker to trace the desired shape of the twin Devil's tails onto

Though we were fairly far along in our West Coast Chopper project, chief builder Steve Peffer had a brainstorm that had to be seen to be believed.

And like most chopper details it started with a piece of steel sheet stock and a torch.

the sheet metal piece which was about ½ inch thick with an outside measurement of about 12 x 12 inches. A band saw was used to rough cut an outside shape, followed by some further shaping with a hand grinder. He then used a milling machine to channel a massive V-shaped slot in the bottom of each of the Devil tails so they could be easily welded in place over the frame rails. A long session with the putty knife followed, as both tails were covered in Bondo and smoothed until they merged seamlessly with the chassis itself.

We had briefly considered performing similar surgery on the rear fender, which can easily be improved upon and personalized with designs cut into its sides and rear lip. The Jesse James fenders are famously strong and include welded-in steel support bracing running underneath so there's little to compromise the structural integrity of one of these babies unless a truly radical amount of metal is removed. Instead, we decided to leave the fenders alone and focus on detailing other parts of our chopper.

As Steve painstakingly molding the two-piece Devil tails in place to appear as if they came from the factory this way, we started looking for other areas of our kit bike to improve upon. It's details like these that builders of name-brand choppers can add on to make a Paul Yaffe, Jesse James, or Chica bike more original rather than just creating a chopper that mimics something already done by the builders themselves. And best of all, besides a few extra hours of labor (OK, quite a few) the fabricated Devil tails didn't cost a cent to construct as they were made from scrap metal and Bondo we'd used to smooth out the sheet metal parts.

In the past, Steel City's Choppers have created some industry-leading special parts like detachable kickstarters that double as brass knuckles (for strictly decorative purposes, of course) and solo seat suspension systems for hardtail bikes built from the vulcanized air shocks on Cannondale mountain bicycles. An EL Knucklehead Harley-Davidson built at the shop even includes an electric starter mated to a late-model five-speed transmission and set of footpegs shaped like dog bones.

This time, Steve had a vision of a set of footpegs made to resemble oversized engine mounting bolts. Using a lathe, he cut a length of stainless-steel rod with ¾-inch coarse threads and hex-milled the bolts' crown on a milling machine. Section of smaller threads cut to feed into the peg mounting holes on

One of the signature details of motorcycles built at *Steve's Steel City Choppers* is a wicked, pointed Devil tail—our rigid C.F.L. was to receive one for each of the axle covers. Steve Dietz

An angle grinder was employed to create angled edges to the tails, while a channel was cut that would allow space for the frame to slot into. Steve Dietz

As Steve shaped the sheet metal for the twin Devil tails, he was preparing to re-mold and repaint the rear end of the chassis—sometimes genius costs time and money!

Here, shop body expert Jared applies several thick layers of Bondo to the frame's axle junctions after Steve has welded the Devil tails into place.

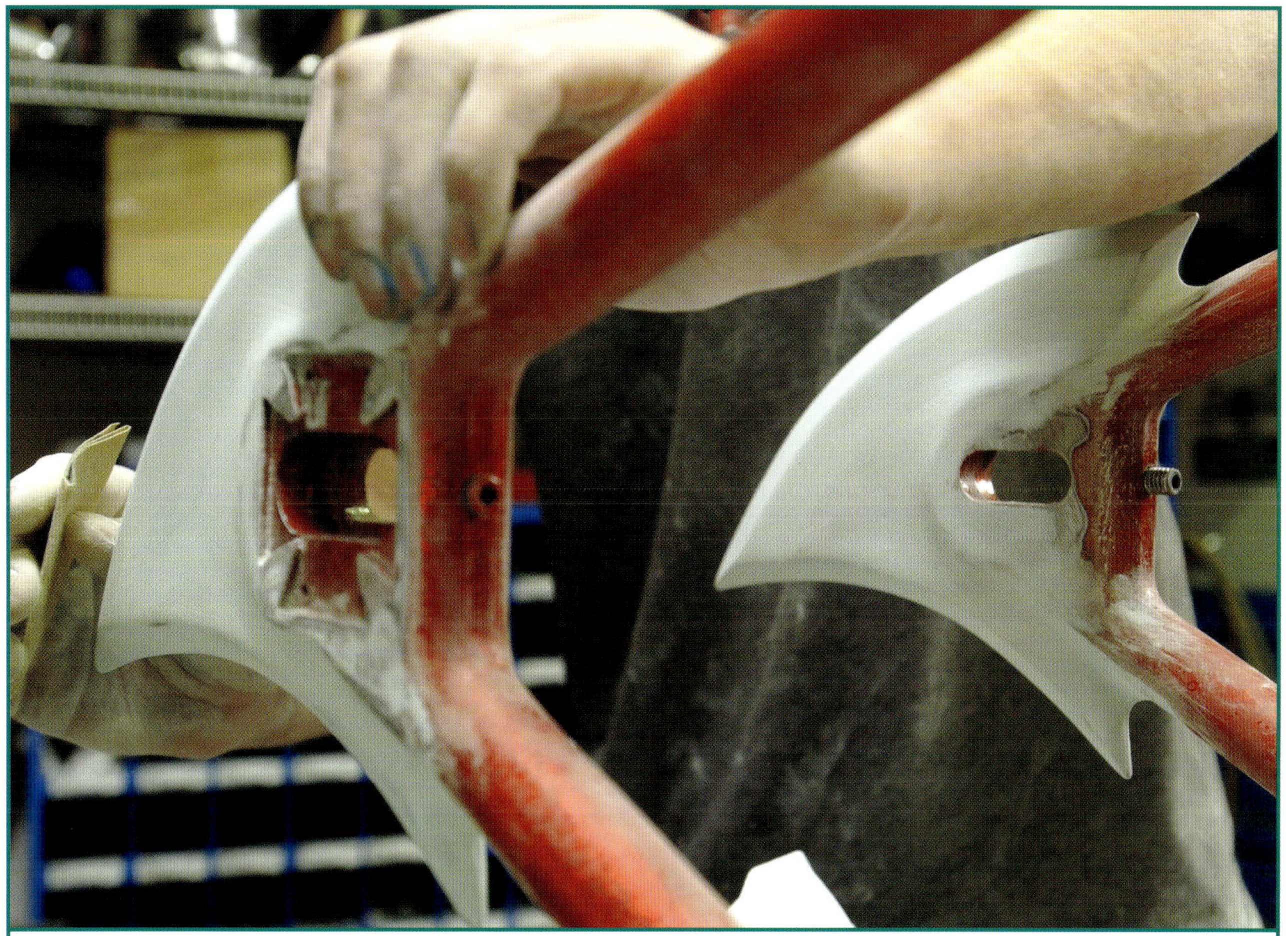

Note the holes for the stock West Coast Chopper Maltese cross axle covers cut into the new tail section. The modification added a good half-week's labor to the project, but details like these make a homemade chopper your own.

our Ness Radius forward controls was made after taking a careful inside thread measurement. Next, the pegs were polished on a simple rotary buffer, the threads filed clean, and on they went.

Our builder was on a roll now, and determined to make this machine a show-winner without raising our basic construction budget by more than a few dollars at a time. He pulled the lead wire connecting the CCI chromed headlamp and replaced it with a quirky-looking piece of coiled red wire, color-matched to the rest of the motorcycle, that he'd found, naturally, inside a discarded telephone. This tiny and relatively simple modification was the sort of thing that bike show judges really appreciate and required little more than the removal of the gas tank and the splicing in of a single wire to the harness.

And speaking of the gas tank, early on in our project, Steve had toyed with the idea of focusing the theme of this motorcycle on gambling. He's envisioned a paint scheme with oversized playing cards decorating the tank and flowing over the frame tubing, but those plans were somehow lost along the way. But being an inveterate pack rat, the builder had managed to find a set of oversized gaming dice which he drilled and tapped to use as an accent piece on our West Coast Chopper. We found the perfect place for them after noticing how the gas tank's Frisco-style mounts leave the front attaching bolts too prominently exposed—a headless double-threaded bolt and some Loc-Tite later and we were rollin' high style.

Had the Perse Performance front end not been designed with hidden axles, we would have continued the theme with axle bolts as well, though future modifications will involve dice-shaped valve stem caps and, if we can manage it, we'll mount a set to our license plate as well. Much later while we were on a fluids run

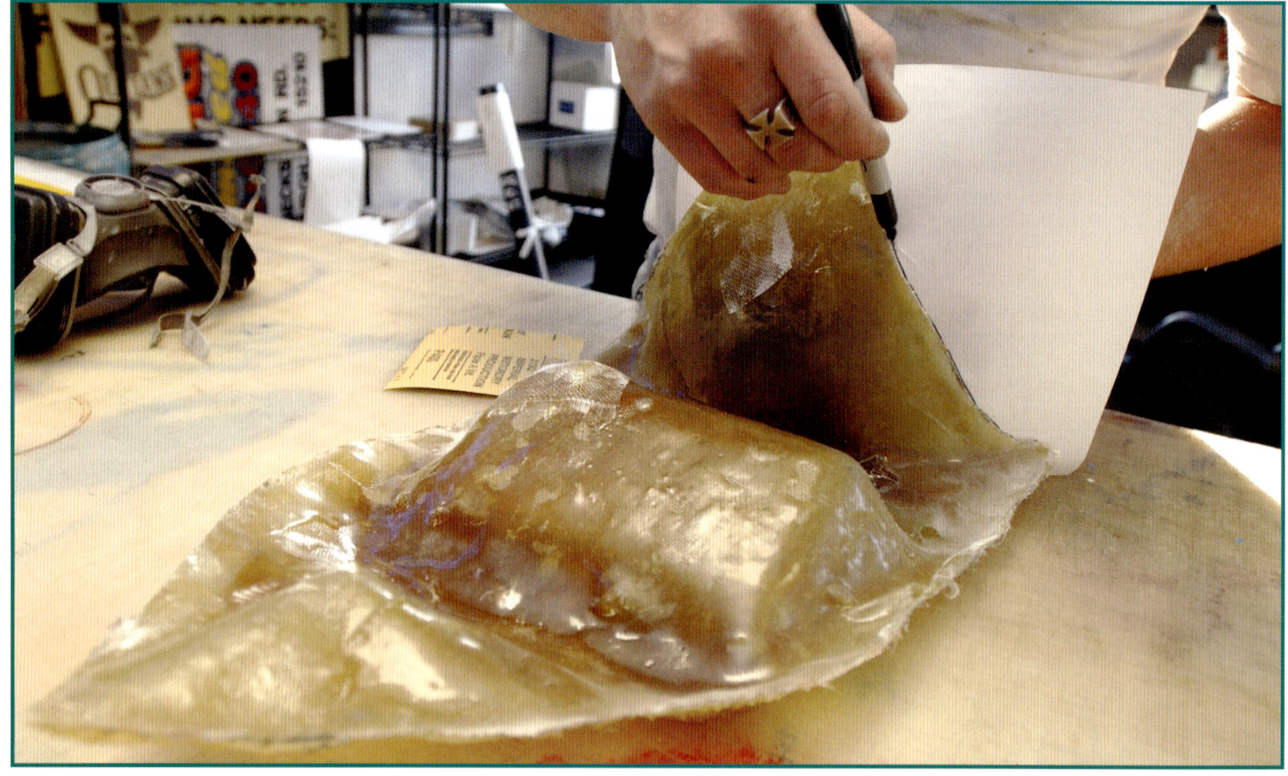

Laying down the custom-poured fiberglass seat pan. Note the extra large hump to leave room for the chopper's oversized battery.

Previous and above: A fiberglass casting was taken of the battery compartment and space where the handmade seat would be mounted; once hardened, the pan was taken to Matt Maroni of M.P.M. Customs who fashioned a Velcro mounting strap system to the pan and added a thick foam pad and black leather upholstery with a red-stitched spiderweb pattern—nice!

to a local auto parts store, Steve picked up a small chromed skull shift knob for $20, the kind of cheap accent piece that's used by import compact car fans to trick-out their Mazda Miatas and Ford Mustangs.

We held on to the chromed skull with its battery-operated glowing red eyes until Steve had another brainstorm—this time involving a power shifter for the chopper's five-speed transmission. As someone who has scared himself pretty well learning to ride a chopper equipped with a jockey shifter, I had no interest in equipping my own chopper with one of these heart-stopping devices. But Steve, as a big fan of the laid-back riding position afforded chopper riders utilizing the foot-clutch/hand shifter combination, had a solution: The slap-shifter, as he calls it. This is basically an extra length of chromed shifter linkage con-

necting a 14-inch steel arm to the existing shifter rod. This allows the rider to power shift the transmission (without the clutch being engaged, which would be impossible with one hand on the throttle and the other using the shifter knob) for forward gears only, while looking tremendously outlaw-cool.

The Steel City Choppers crew spent about eight hours fabricating a shifter rod for the slap-shifter from a piece of square, $1/2$-inch stock. Heated with an acetylene torch until glowing red, the shaft was slowly twisted with four sets of hands and assistance from a set of oversized pliers until it had the swirling contours of one of those old 1960s springer front forks. This, we must warn, is not a task for the casual hobbyist bike builder or those unfamiliar with high-end forge and machine shop work. Once mastered, the art of metal-

Flush-mounted gas cap is key-activated and a W.C.C. exclusive - logo is a vinyl sticker and cost just a couple of bucks.

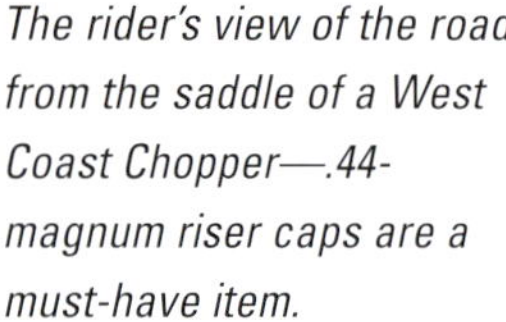

The rider's view of the road from the saddle of a West Coast Chopper—.44-magnum riser caps are a must-have item.

Weld's Widow wheels with matching chrome billet brake rotors were a smart choice.

Moderate in its stretch and rake, the C.F.L. chopper is stubby compared to many of the custom bikes emerging from today's custom shops. This means it will ride as sharp as it looks.

Hell bent exhaust pipes make the 113-cubic-inch motor sing on note, but you may want to invest in a set of internal baffles after checking with your local authorities—these babies are LOUD!

Front master cylinder from G.M.A. looks coolly understated in anodized clear finish—we'd considered having it anodized in red to match the bike but opted not to.

Builder Steve Peffer deserved much props for creating a show-stopping chopper for about one-third the cost of having one custom built to order by Jesse James himself: check out the Devil mascot, thumbing his nose at convention. Steve found this part at a car salvage yard and had it chromed.

Rear drive chain visible between the frame rails—flawless paint reflects nicely on the engine's factory-installed chrome plating.

Expert upholsterer Matt Maroni of M.P.M. Customs from Pittsburgh created this plus chopper solo saddle from a custom-molded fiberglass seat pan— cheaper options are available, but not as nice.

Above: Oversize dice installed on the upper tank mounts add a sense of mischief to our chopper; braided gas lines are a cool, 1960s chopper touch. Left: Side-mounted license plate frame is from Pro-One and includes an integral taillight and bolts directly to the belt primary drive housing.

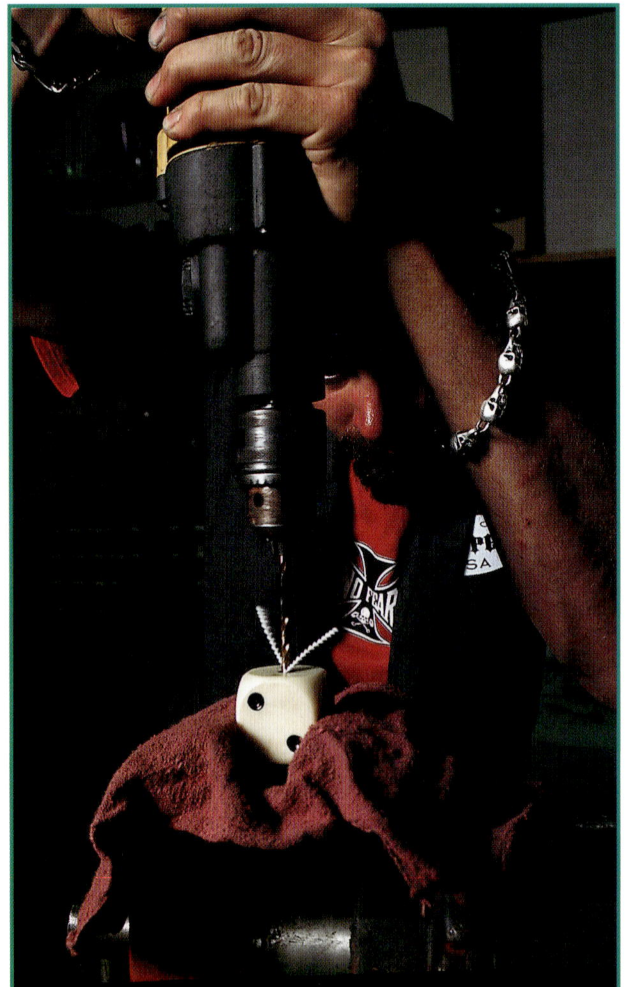

Here, Steve drills and taps the giant gaming dice that were mounted to the gas tank for a wild visual effect. Found items like these don't cost a fortune and can really make your chopper memorable. Joe Appel

wrending can yield all sorts of cool parts like twisted handlebars and sissy bars and fender struts, but for the few dollars it costs to have an experienced metalsmith perform this work for you—compared to the high risk of failure (or worse yet, burns!)—it's best not to try this at home. Of course, Steve had the necessary experience, and after the piece was allowed to cool overnight, he then drilled a small channel down the length of the rod, and had it show chrome plated. One end was tapped for the attachment of the skull shifter knob while the other was ground and tapered to fit over a bushing on the transmission shifter rod. A wire was run through the drilled channel, allowing the skull's eyes to glow a fiery red whenever the gear shifter is used. Again, the costs of this modification were less than $200 including chrome plating of the shifter rod,

which is not much for the sort of custom detailing that really makes a chopper stand out from the crowd.

I'd initially opted to save bucks by using an off-the-shelf aftermarket solo saddle. Firms like Mustang, LePera, Corbin, and others all manufacture well-made genuine leather seats or hardtail frames, but we received an offer from one Matt Maroni, proprietor of M.P.M. Customs, who volunteered to craft a one-off seat for us from scratch. Matt works almost exclusively with custom chopper fabricators, molding seat pans from either aluminum or fiberglass, and cutting seat cushions that can include either straight foam or gel pads for long-range comfort on hardtail choppers. Ours was comprised of a fiberglass pan made by heating up a hand-cut section of fiberglass sheeting until it was pliable and pressing it over the frame and bat-

Tapped and threaded internally, the dice mount with a double-threaded bolt. Joe Appel

The Jesse James front fender all painted, clear coated and mounted—a set of small spacers were purchased from West Coast Choppers to ensure a snug fit with our Wide Glide front forks.

Detail shot of the painted and molded Devil tail after being meticulously welded into place on our rigid frame—careful angle grinding and design means they clear the rear wheel easily.

Welding as an art form—Steve Peffer declines to go aftermarket with many parts and decides to hand-weld a set of angled Z-bars himself. Joe Appel

We'd spent our custom paint budget on a bitchin' red metalflake and flames job, but still wanted to make a statement; ImageWorks, UK crafts stickers like these wacky lettering kits for a few bucks each.

As our project progressed, the ideas just kept flowing; these oversized bolts are made from stainless steel and once polished and threaded to match our Arlen Ness forward controls, they make excellent footpegs.

Detail shot of the mad skull slap-shifter that Steve perfected for our West Coast Chopper; while I was in no hurry to own a motorcycle with an actual jockey shifter, this contraption actually lends a bike the timeless chopper cool of a suicide clutch, while still operating via the hand-shift mechanism.

tery compartment. With that template hardened by the next day, Maroni cut a section of padding measured to fit the space and stitched a leather seat cover with a funky little spiderweb design—in red, to match the rest of our chopper's detailing. Had we paid full retail, the M.P.M. custom seat (which is stuffed full for my considerable girth—thanks Matt!) would have cost about $450 or so. With only a week or so between order date and delivery, M.P.M. offers a great deal for a unique accent piece for a homemade chopper.

The Steel City Choppers crew gave me the impression that they could have continued making their amazing detail changes to our project chopper all month. They'd even unearthed a very sinister-looking antique chrome Devil hood ornament at a car parts swap that was ceremoniously welded atop the coil spacer and, one day, a script of stick-on vinyl lettering appeared along the frame's lower rail declaring "Pimpin' Ain't Easy" to the world. But we had finally finished the build process and I, for one, was eager to get our C.F.L. on the road.

RIDING IMPRESSION

For riders not intimately involved with choppers on the street, it's quite an eye-opener to finally crank the throttle on a low-riding motorcycle with twice the torque and all the horsepower of today's liter-sized sportbikes. It wasn't exactly a matter of popping in the

Chromed skull shift knob works in forward gears only; glowing red eyes are way cool in any era; cost? About $20 from our local auto parts store plus handmade shifter linkage.

DO'S AND DON'TS

DO: Look in strange places for accent pieces for your chopper. Old car hood ornaments make excellent fender trim and swap meets are brimming with potential custom goodies.

DON'T: Worry about what everybody else thinks—this is your chopper, so build it your way.

ignition key and pressing a starter button as you would on a stock motorcycle. Each of the chopper's individual components has to be tested by riding the bike for short runs before any real distance riding can be attempted.

The Midwest engine was no exception. It included instructions that were comprehensive and detailed about the complex, first-time starting procedure that involved cranking the engine over for several brief cycles and rapidly cooling the fins with a high-speed fan. The head bolts and oil lines required checking and re-torquing for each of the five- to fifteen-minute test sessions we ran before rolling our kit bike onto the streets for the first time. A note to the wise: The blue compression-release pins clearly visible just behind the spark plugs MUST be clicked down before cranking the starter button lest you burn out a starter unit (that's $250 to you and me). We also used the first starting sessions to adjust final free play in the throttle cables, adjusting the idle on the S&S "D" carburetor by ear as the C.F.L. was running no tachometer.

Expect to tinker with and fine-tune your chopper for the first 100 miles or so, as new parts will need a few miles to fully break in as the machine's tolerances settle in. If you haven't ridden a hardtail chopper before, expect some fairly lazy around-town steering, and a highway ride that's as stable as a high-speed Amtrak shuttle. A motor with 113 cubic inches of displacement churns out most of its 120 foot-pounds of torque right off idle, so it's easy to accidentally spin the rear tire if you're not careful with the throttle. This may be great for impressing groups of high school kids walking down the road, but absolutely terrifying if you don't know what to expect. With no rear suspension, we definitely recommend using a fully telescoping front end like our Perse Performance unit. And the multi-piston brakes, like our GMA models, were a great choice as these bikes can build up some serious three-figure speeds without the rider really noticing how fast they're traveling.

After the first few miles, check and, if necessary, tighten every bolt including the battery connectors, all shifter linkage, the drive chain, and check the tension in the primary belt drive according to the specs laid out in the Primo instruction booklet. Unlike choppers of old, reliability is not much of an issue for today's custom motorcycles, whether they were built within the confines of a celebrity builder's shop, or at home by a competent mechanic. Most of the custom chopper builders we spoke with during the research for this book and project had experienced small problems with individual components such as electrical parts or carburetors. Don't be shocked to find the occasional loose bolt on your solidly connected parts like handlebar risers, exhaust pipes, and fenders. But we heard little of the cracked frames, non-working brakes, and rickety wheels that made chopper riding such a manly endeavor a couple of decades ago. Still, we can't stress too heartily the need to do your homework, checking over your chopper for any loose nuts and bolts before and after every ride. Rigid-mounted engines and transmissions can throw an awful lot of vibration to the far reaches of your motorcycle, as can speed bumps, potholes, and every other obstacle modern highways have to offer. That means routine maintenance is a no-brainer, even if it means simply checking your tire pressures, drive chain tension, and fluid levels on a weekly basis to make sure there are no surprises in store for you or your chopper in the passing lane.

And be sure to enjoy yourself; soaking up the admiring glances and envious stares of all the people who haven't yet invested the time, imagination, money, and sweat in creating their own West Coast Chopper is the best part.

COST COMPARISONS

While this chopper project was undertaken with a theme of affordability in mind, we refused to skimp when it came time to select several major components. A West Coast Chopper running a set of cheap, aftermarket exhaust pipes and a swap meet chassis just wouldn't accomplish our goal of trying to re-create what they do so well out in Long Beach.

Because the disposable income most chopper builders have to invest in a custom bike varies wildly, we attempted to run our project West Coast Chopper right down the median—the grand total for the parts we used came to just under $34,000 at full retail. While this is far from a small amount of money, by anyone's standards, when viewed in contrast to the price of a late-model stock Harley-Davidson Big Twin, it really isn't what you could call extravagant, either. What we invested was about equal to the mid-level price you'd pay in today's market for an assembly-line custom chopper or lowrider from the likes of Big Dog, Texas Chopper, or any of the popular "clone" motorcycle manufacturers.

For this investment, an at-home builder can have their dream chopper built to their exact specifications concerning paint, performance, and whatever accessories they choose to employ. The custom touches that have made our project bike a show-stopper actually cost very little and can be found in any shopping mall auto parts store or improved out of leftover bits found at any motorcycle swap meet or custom parts dealership. And there's little chance of us running into someone else with an exact replica of our West Coast Chopper anytime soon.

Best of all, we could have easily created a unique, crowd-pleasing chopper for a considerably smaller sum using parts and major components that cost less. Check out the following price comparison chart and consider where you might want to cut corners when hitting the workbench yourself.

ENGINE
Top-Shelf: Midwest El Bruto 113-cubic-inch, $6,800
Bargain: Harley-Davidson Evolution 80-cubic-inch from West Virginia H-D, $2,700

FORKS
Top-Shelf: Perse Performance Hex-leg Wide Glide, $2,900
Bargain: CCI single-disc FXWG style front end, $749

FORWARD CONTROLS
Top-Shelf: Ness Radius, $1,000
Bargain: CCI Chrome, $225

SEAT
Top-Shelf: Custom Made seat pan with hand-stitched seat leather from M.P.M. Customs, $500
Bargain: Mustang Fastback seat for rigid frames, $243

WHEELS
Top-Shelf: Weld Evo Billet wheels, chromed, $2,100 (per set)
Bargain: Rev Tech wire wheels, $900 (per set)

Using a combination of these and other bargain parts and accessories, a budget-minded chopper builder could easily bring home a smart-looking, bad-assed West Coast Chopper of their own for around $19,000—or easily what lots of riders invest in their Softails only to end up with motorcycles that, to quote Jesse James, "get lost in the parking lot." Because the C.F.L. chassis is designed to accept most parts from a stock Harley-Davidson Softail, Harley-Davidson dealerships could prove invaluable sources for brakes, belt drives, transmissions, and other second-hand parts discarded by Softail owners who are upgrading their own machines.

The choice is yours—happy shopping.

BUDGET CHOPPER BUILD RESOURCE GUIDE

M.P.M. Customs
Custom Made Seats
208 Main Street
Tarentum, PA 15084
(724) 226-8534
www.mpmcustoms@aol.com

Steel City Choppers
Custom paint, building, and complete sheet metal fabrication services. Nationwide shipping available.
107 Freeport Road
Butler, PA 16002
(724) 283-6969
www.steelcitychoppers.com

West Coast Choppers
C.F.L. frame kit, gas tank, and fenders, Hell Bent exhaust pipes, Maltese cross air cleaner, .44-Magnum handlebar risers, and parts to complete your own Jesse James kit bike.
718 West Anaheim Street
Long Beach, CA 90813
(562) 983-6666
www.westcoastchoppers.com

Midwest Motorcycle Supply
El Bruto 113-cubic-inch polished billet motors from Ultima featuring forged pistons with 10.2: 1 compression, billet oil pump, .625 lift cam, and S&S "D" series carburetor—punching out 120 rear-wheel horsepower and 120 foot-pounds of torque(!)
P.O. Box 499
Arnold, MO 63010
www.midwest-mc.com or 800-325-3914

Perse Performance
Black chrome FXWG hex front end with 41-mm tubes, Race Tech springs and oils, Gold Valve cartridge emulators, hidden axles and brake line routings, and adjustable preload.
10577 West Centennial Rd.
Littleton, CO 80127
(817) 631-3093
www.perseperformance.com

GMA Engineering
Brake calipers, master cylinders, hand and foot controls.
13526 A Street
Omaha, NE 68144
(402) 334-5105
www.gmabrakes.com

Weld Racing
"Widow" rims from Weld's Evo series, custom CNC milled wheels made from virgin 6061 aircraft-grade aluminum, matching brake rotors and belt pulleys. Chromed wheels have a complete, five-year warranty.
933 Mulberry Street
Kansas City, MO 64101
www.evomotorcycle.com or 866-753-4284

Custom Chrome, Inc.
Ness Tech forward controls, braided steel oil and brake lines, Primo five–inch open belt drive system, chrome kickstand, five-inch headlight.
www.customchrome.com or 800-729-3332

PPG Industries
Body filler, primer.

Colorite Industries
Paints.
National Sales Office
11603 Groveland Ave.
Whittier, CA 90604
sales@color-rite.com or 800-736-7980
Fax: 661-266-0286